PROJECTS ON PURPOSE

Mark D. Steele

PROJECTS <u>ON PURPOSE</u>

MARK D. STEELE

Old Elm Tree Press
Exton, Pennsylvania

OLD ELM TREE PRESS
FIRST EDITION JUNE 2017

Library of Congress Control Number: 2017908978
ISBN: 978-0-692-84123-5

ACKNOWLEDGEMENTS

Thanks to my friend and past co-author, John Pourdehnad, for always being a willing sounding board for my ideas on the application of systems thinking to project management and for being a beta reader.

Thanks to my friend Jason Magidson (Author of *Engaged: Creating a Great Organization through Extraordinary Employee and User Engagement*) for providing the foundation for the chapter on Idealized Design as well for encouragement and our "accountability meetings" along the way and, finally, for his detailed and invaluable feedback on my draft.

Thanks to my friend and former co-instructor Ann Tomalavage for her thoughts and encouragement and for her feedback on the risk management portions in particular.

Thanks to those who provided encouragement along the way as well as my group of beta readers who provided invaluable feedback: Brad Kelley, Gerri Iseman, Karl Hamilton, Steve Carroll, Stephen Titus, and Susan Grumer. All of these people have made this book better. Any flaws are my own.

And thanks especially to Russell L. Ackoff (1919 - 2009), the late systems thinker and teacher for his brilliant contributions to the field of systems thinking and its application to organizations of all types.

TABLE OF CONTENTS

Introduction

The goal of this book is to distill a mash of twenty-nine years of getting things done, a healthy dose of organizational systems theory, and real-world experience in the analysis of failed projects (usually for litigation) into a smooth shot glass of advice on how to take your projects to the next level. My purpose is nothing less than to revolutionize project management by presenting you with a challenge disguised as a book, by combining the passion of a business manifesto with a "how to" on creating successful projects.

This book is short but the ideas are big. I suspect that you have also seen too many problem projects as well or you would not have read even this far. If so, this book should provide you with more than one "aha" moment. But do not just read. Think about, expand upon, and tailor these ideas to your project. Know where you want to go and get there. Do your projects on purpose.

Each project exists for a unique purpose. If you could turn out the desired result on an assembly line, then you would not need to set up a project. This is true whether the project involves the integration of software for a major corporation or the construction of a new building. In each case, you are reinventing the wheel. And while each wheel might share characteristics with previous wheels, your project needs a wheel that is, at least in some important way, unique.

Projects fail. And traditional project management methods and techniques are not really designed to make projects successful. When I see the way in which some projects are set up, I think of the children's excuse, "But it wasn't my fault. I didn't do it on purpose." I wonder if leadership would also make excuses, saying, "But we didn't do it on purpose."

Do organizations actually do projects on purpose? And, if not, why not? If you are going to spend all of that time, money, and effort on your project, don't you think you should at least be "on purpose"? You must be thinking, "of course they do." In my consulting role, I have had the opportunity to study and analyze a lot of projects ranging from relatively small to really large, big-name projects (multi-billion dollars in some cases) and I have reluctantly reached a number of conclusions:

1. **Many projects seem designed to fail.** Competing agendas built into the very fabric of the project organization and reinforced through contracts and systems of incentives and disincentives ultimately and predictably tear the project apart. I have analyzed projects that made me wonder if leadership even wanted the project to succeed.

2. **Projects do not lack focus. They focus in the wrong direction.** Because of this false focus, they often sub-optimize key decisions leading to massive but predictable project failure. Early in the project, corporate and project leadership tend to focus on a series of approvals, whether regulatory or board level, self-congratulatory, and PR rather than the project itself.

3. Even those who incorporate project management "best practices" may find that those practices are not enough. "Best practices" tend to focus on controlling the schedule, the budget, and work quality. Project management, as it is typically understood, is task-focused. But why is this? **<u>People</u> make projects effective and the most critical**

success factors for projects are people-centric (e.g. teamwork and trust). So why emphasize the critical path and project accounting?

Organizations tend to stumble into their projects. They don't have their eye on the ball – instead they are watching the crowd, the weather, the referee, or the scoreboard. Their projects are not on purpose. This problem points to an obvious solution. Organizations should actually do projects on purpose. But what would such an approach look like? How would such a project differ from typical projects? And would it work?

Meeting the schedule and the budget should be merely the most basic rungs on the ladder of project success. Organizations need projects that unleash creativity, energy, and potential. A successful project should enhance not only the bottom line but also an organization's brand, its reputation for quality, and the human factors essential for organizational effectiveness. A project should engender more excitement than anxiety, more buzz than gossip and more awe than derision among the organization's members, customers, competitors, and communities.

Most writing on project management tells you how it has been done before. The purpose of this book is to open your eyes to ways in which projects can be designed to be more effective, more exciting, more inspiring, and, ultimately, more successful.

This book is divided into five parts:

- **Part 1, The Project Mess**, discusses the paradox of modern project management and why its tools and techniques do not lead to greater success.
- **Part 2, Project Challenges**, describes the various categories and types of challenges faced by project teams as they attempt to make their projects successful. These challenges include hidden agendas and assumptions, complexity factors, and risks from the outside.
- **Part 3, Projects as Social Systems**, explains the background and key elements of systems thinking vis-à-vis project organizations and the major implications of that approach.
- **Part 4, Designing Project Success**, lays out the seven critical design principles for projects derived from systems thinking.
- **Part 5, Tools for Success**, discusses other aspects of a systems approach and some of innovative ways in which it might be applied to your project through participative team

selection, the idealized design process, re-imagined project controls, the targeting approach, and design visualization.

Part 1
The Project
Mess

"Would you tell me, please, which way I ought to go from here?"
"That depends a good deal on where you want to get to," said the Cat.
"I don't much care where--" said Alice.
"Then it doesn't matter which way you go," said the Cat.
"--so long as I get SOMEWHERE," Alice added as an explanation.
"Oh, you're sure to do that," said the Cat, "if you only walk long enough."

--- Lewis Carroll, Alice in Wonderland

Part 1 – The Project Mess

The first part of Dr. Russell Ackoff's systems approach is to understand the "Mess".[1] Ackoff defined a mess as a set of interrelated and interacting problems. In this case, we are discussing project management as a whole and, in this part, I am going to explain why a significant paradox exists in the modern project management world and how modern project management techniques are not enough to cause project success.

Messes are interesting "creatures." There is an ancient tale of a knot in Egypt referred to as the Gordian knot. It was a rope so knotted and tangled that nobody had been able to untie it. In fact, the prophecy stated that whomever untied the knot would rule all of Asia. Legend has it that Alexander the Great visited this site. His ambitions extended across Asia and he was intrigued by the prophecy. He took one look at the knot, made even messier and more tangled by generations of attempts to untie it. He then drew his sword and, in one deft stroke, cut the knot in half. Did that technically fulfil the prophecy? Who knows? Alexander did go on to conquer much of Asia extending into what is now Afghanistan and India.

But for our purposes that knot is analogous to the Mess. Systems thinking ultimately teaches us ways to look beyond the mess and see the forest for the trees. It teaches us to identify the ultimate goal or purpose and then to cut through the tangled knot.

1. The Project Management Paradox

A paradox exists when two statements appear contradictory yet both seem to be true. Of course, contradictions cannot actually exist so what is really going on in the case of a paradox is that either the understanding of the two statements is incomplete or there is some hidden assumption that connects the two. The world of project management is a paradox. On one side, interest in and expenditures for project management techniques, methods, organizations, and training are increasing and more organizations are employing these practices while on the other side projects tend to fail on a regular basis. Of course, the hidden assumption that connects these two statements is that the project management interest, techniques, training, etc. should lead to improved project performance. I believe that this assumption is false most of the time. This section provides more background on the paradox.

The flip side of the paradox is that projects continue to fail at a high rate. Failure means that one or more significant business objectives are not met. These objectives may relate to the project budget, schedule, scope of work, or quality but often show up as a complex set of interacting problems. Failures may also arise due to events outside the control of the project management staff or any of the involved parties. A failed project will typically be behind schedule, over budget, or, often more critically, will have decreased scope from that originally planned due to schedule or budget pressures.

For decades, the literature has supported the idea that projects as a whole are **not** becoming more successful.

2. Project Failure is Common

The Project Management Institute (PMI) defines a project as:

a temporary endeavor undertaken to create a unique product or service[2]

What is project failure? Failure means that one or more significant business objectives are not met (i.e. the "temporary" endeavor was not as temporary as planned, or it cost more, or the final unique product or service did not match expectations). These objectives may relate to the project budget, schedule, scope of work, quality, or safety but often show up as a complex set of interacting problems. Failures may also arise due to events outside the control of the project management staff or any of the involved parties.

Project failures are not new and do not seem to be disappearing. The French project to complete a canal across the Panamanian isthmus failed in the late 1800's. Examples since then abound but more recent studies illustrate that project failures in terms of scope, quality, budget, or schedule may not be rare:

- Repeated studies report that final project costs on airport construction tend to be about 1/3 higher than the planned costs.[3]

- A study of 52 large-scale private projects showed an average cost overrun of 88% and time overrun of 17%. In addition, only half of the completed projects met performance expectations.[4]

- A report from the United Kingdom found that construction projects ranging from hospitals to roads had average schedule overruns of 11% and cost overruns of 14%.[5]

- A report evaluating international development projects funded by the World Bank stated that more "than a third of the IDA [International Development Association] and IBRD [International Bank for Reconstruction and Development] projects most recently evaluated by the Bank itself were rated 'unsatisfactory'."[6]

- A process industry study found that "...more than two-thirds of major projects built by the process industries in the United States in the past five years has failed to meet one or more of the key objectives anticipated at authorization."[7]
- An international report on large-scale dam projects stated that they generally experience schedule delay and budget overruns and fail to perform to expectations.[8]
- PwC reviewed over 10,000 projects (presumably mostly IT projects) from 200 companies in 30 countries across various industries and found that only 2.5% of the companies successfully completed 100% of their projects.[9]
- "A study published in the Harvard Business Review, which analyzed 1,471 IT projects, found that the average overrun was 27%, but one in six projects had a cost overrun of 200% on average and a schedule overrun of almost 70%."[10]
- Ernst & Young reviewed 365 projects in the oil and gas sector with project values of $1 billion or greater and found that 64% were facing cost overruns and 73% were facing schedule delays.[11]

Some of the most dramatic (and expensive) project failures can be found in the construction sector across many industries – transportation, power generation, heavy industry, commercial, and healthcare. The prevalence of the project management focus within the construction industry (and relatively early adoption of project management methods, in some cases decades earlier than other industries) makes these failures especially distressing. But the construction industry is far from alone.

Information technology (IT) and other projects face similar problems. A commonly quoted statistic among IT projects is that only one-third of them finish on time. One report on product development projects stated that 30% of them score low in terms of meeting their business objectives. And government procurement projects, such as those funded by the Department of Defense, experience massive overruns, poor results, and incredible schedule delays as the norm rather than the exception – whether submarines, new fighter jets, fighting vehicles, or field gear.

I have been following the statistics on project success and failure for twenty years and could probably drown you with statistics that paint a bleak picture. But you probably would not have read this far if you had not experienced problem projects or, at least, heard enough about them to be concerned for your own projects. Clearly the causes may vary, but, taken together, they do not speak well for the effectiveness of project management as currently understood and applied. Many project personnel and organizational leaders have faced problems with scope, budget, schedule, or project dilution in which scope is sacrificed to meet a budget or schedule to enable the company to proclaim an early victory – often to the dissatisfaction of those left with the project results.

Project failure shows up in a variety of ways:

- Excessive cost. And this does not relate merely to budget. That is possibly just a failure of prediction. The goal is to get more value for less cost. Compared to that goal, paying more than you needed to is a failure (even if you come in under budget).
- Late schedule: Taking longer than necessary is a failure.
- Reductions in scope during design and early construction phases leading in order to make scope or budget.
- Excessive change orders during construction.
- Contract defaults.
- Failure to operate as planned once complete: When the project or significant parts of it do

not work or cannot be used for its intended purpose.

- Unreliability or lack of durability.
- Unsatisfied stakeholders.
- Disputes or litigation.

3. Proliferation of "Project Management"

While projects continue to fail two other trends are also occurring: the proliferation of project management tools, techniques, and solutions and the *projectization* of the workplace.

Project management is gaining in popularity. For example, the Project Management Institute (PMI), has seen its membership increase from 8,500 in 1990 to over 2.9 million members as of the beginning of 2017 with over 650,000 active Project Management Professionals (PMPs).[12] Project management "trend-watchers" have stated that project management "is one of the fastest growing, widely recognized trends of the last decade." In addition, the number of project management organizations, journals, certifications, books, training courses, and degree programs appears to be steadily rising.

What I refer to as *projectization* involves the spread of the project management gospel into organizations that one might not traditionally think of as "project" organizations (e.g. banking, education, and other sectors). More organizations are turning to project management methods and tools to manage a variety of work efforts.

The projectization trend benefits from and also feeds into the proliferation of project management demonstrated by dramatic increases in types and quantities of project management organizations, software, solutions, training, academic programs, certifications, and media including books, journals, and other forms.

These two trends, the increase in project management resources and the projectization of the workplace, are tied together and feed off of each other.

The problem is that this proliferation of tools and techniques may not be helping to improve project performance. The Hoover Dam project, completed in 1936, achieved a high level of success for its day in terms of its challenging scope of work, the innovation involved in accomplishing that scope, and the fact that the project finished within its schedule and budgetary constraints even though not one computer packed with the latest project management software was available.

Mark Twain, in Life on the Mississippi, said that there "is something fascinating about science. One gets such wholesome returns of conjecture out of such a trifling investment of fact."

Mark Twain's observation about science might also apply to modern project management tools. They enable the project management or controls team to arrive at minutely detailed forecasts, schedules, and budgets but do not necessarily provide a way to get the job done. In fact, the focus on forecasts might itself be an issue as the ability to predict the future is much sought after but rarely if ever seen. One recent paper discussed similar problems with the prevalence of management gurus and fads altogether. It proposed that the proliferation of techniques and tools do not often lead to success because the tools themselves are not capable of influencing success.[13]

The techniques and methodologies do not completely lack value but are not enough. Many project management methods fall into a category that philosophers refer to as *necessary but not sufficient*. That is, they are necessary for project management but they, alone, cannot cause project success. But you would never guess that from the marketing.

4. The Elephant in the Project Room

Even with the correct and diligent application of project management techniques and methodologies, projects still fail. In one $200 million project that I analyzed, the engineering and construction firm responsible for the project applied state of the art project controls. The project team tracked project cost data on a continuous basis and could print out cost reports as needed. They updated the project schedules at least two times a month, measured the productivity of the workforce in over 20 different categories on a weekly basis, made detailed use of logs for documents, faxes, and other correspondence including a standardized filing system, AND lost over $50 million on the project. The use of standard project management tools on this project could provide plentiful textbook examples but did not lead to project success. And this project is not alone.

The overall impact of these techniques and methodologies as typically applied is marginal at best. The engineering and construction industry is not seeing the types of gains common to other types of work such as manufacturing. Too often, project management methodologies serve as window dressing for a project that is set up to fail from the beginning. But even when used conscientiously, **the best of project management methods and tools are not <u>designed</u>** to cause project success. Project management techniques usually involve forecasting the results ahead of time and then measuring the results during the project to determine if the project is meeting the forecast. Most project management methods are analogous to predicting the score in a football game and then keeping that score during the game.

Imagine the scene after a football game on Sunday. The coach holds a press conference and, when asked why his team failed, he blames the statisticians and the score keepers. The truth is that the statisticians and the score keepers, while providing useful and sometimes maybe even critical information for decisions, are NOT the reason why the team lost. Whether through flawed decisions, poor execution, bad luck, or just a really tough opponent – the team lost the game, play by play. It lost because it did not score more points than the other team or keep the other team from scoring points against it.

If a computer whiz kid from the local university developed a program that enabled the near perfect prediction of the opponent's score on Sunday, every week, then the coach would know exactly how many points would be needed to win before the game even started. Then the score keepers would keep him apprised of the score as the game progressed. Neither the prediction, nor the current score, actually helps the coach or his team to get the ball into the end zone or through the uprights or to stop the other team from doing so.

Yet what does a typical project management technique do? Let us look at a typical project cost control process. There are all sorts of names for each step so I have tried to keep them generic.

As you can see in the diagram below, this process follows the same path as our sports analogy above: **prediction** – followed by **tracking**. Thus, project cost management, scheduling, and most other project management techniques, are analogous to the score-keeping model. They are not the cause of either project success or project failure. If poorly done they may provide flawed decision-making data but, ultimately, the project team succeeds or fails due to factors other than "score" prediction and "score-keeping". How does score-prediction or score-keeping actually help a

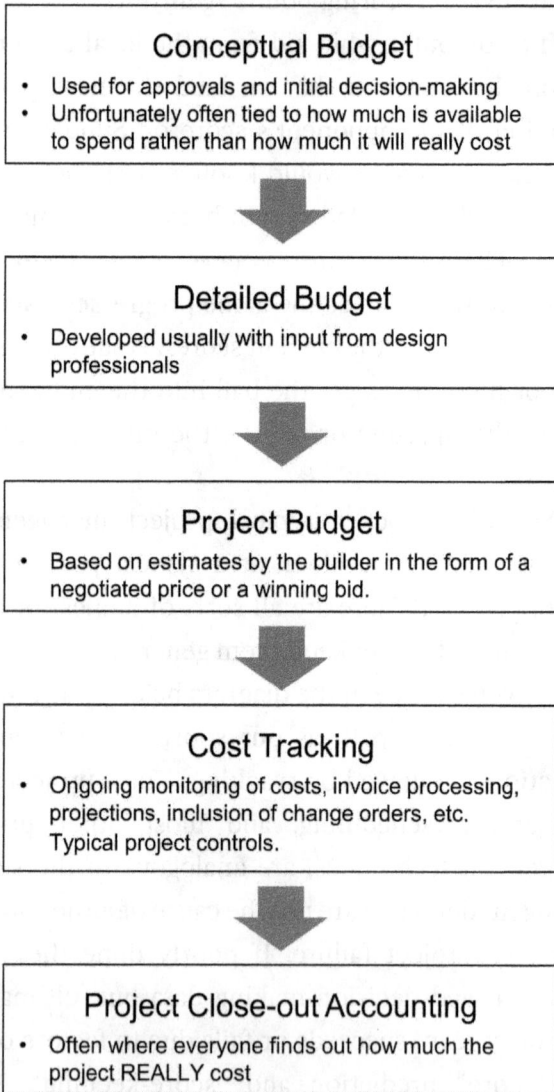

Conceptual Budget

- Used for approvals and initial decision-making
- Unfortunately often tied to how much is available to spend rather than how much it will really cost

Detailed Budget

- Developed usually with input from design professionals

Project Budget

- Based on estimates by the builder in the form of a negotiated price or a winning bid.

Cost Tracking

- Ongoing monitoring of costs, invoice processing, projections, inclusion of change orders, etc. Typical project controls.

Project Close-out Accounting

- Often where everyone finds out how much the project REALLY cost team to score points? They are necessary but not sufficient.

Whenever failure is the rule rather than the exception, a systemic problem is likely the culprit. A systemic problem is one that is built into the very structure or approach being used. Problems in failed projects seem to be systemic and structural rather than partial and local. Systemic and structural problems lead to project failure even when project management techniques are rigorously applied. Often, when project management techniques are not rigorously applied, it is not because the parties do not know that they should be applying them but this failure, like the larger project failure, is brought on by larger systemic problems.

The next section, Part 2, Project Challenges, focuses on many of the systemic problems faced by project teams. It will be followed by Part 3, Projects as Social Systems, which continues this discussion of systemic problems and explains it further in light of systems thinking.

Part 2
Project
Challenges

---

*By the fourth grade, I graduated to an
erector set and spent many happy hours
constructing devices of unknown purpose
where the main design criterion was to
maximize the number of moving
parts and overall size.*
--- Steven Chu

Part 2 – Project Challenges

If we are going to view a project as a system, let us start by looking at the system's environment. The next part of this book will explain what it means to think of a project as system and to take a systems approach to project management. This section of the book, however, might also be called, **The Mess Continued**. In Russell Ackoff's writings, a mess is an interacting set of problems that creates an undesirable outcome or future. An understanding of the very real challenges faced by project teams is just as important as understanding the paradox or the fact that traditional project management techniques do not cause project success. Without understanding the challenges, it will not be easy to understand the ways in which a systems thinking approach can overcome those challenges.

The challenges addressed in this section include competing agendas, hidden assumptions, complexity, and external risks (from outside the project organization).

Have you ever asked yourself the following questions?

1. Are others really on my side in this project?
2. Does X (person or organization) really want this project to succeed?

3. Why didn't we plan for the loss of key project personnel?
4. Who made that decision two years ago and why?
5. Why didn't we see that coming? It seems so unpredictable.
6. What could go wrong that we haven't thought of? And are we ready?

If you have ever asked yourself any of these questions during a project or, if you think that you would rather not be in the position of asking any of them later, then this section is for you.

5. Competing Agendas

Is everybody on your project team really on the same side? When you had your project kick-off meeting, with donuts and coffee, and you all wished the project success, was it all for show? Quite often different project stakeholders have different agendas. What is worse however, is that many times the project is set up in such a way as to encourage competing agendas.

Imagine the following project. An owner wanted to build an interstate fiber optic trunk line. Securing the right of way is a crucial element in the success of any linear project (e.g. communications, pipeline, electrical transmission, etc.). Normally, this activity is measured based on its cost efficiency. In other words, the typical goal is to secure as much right of way as possible for as low a cost as possible. There contracted firms that specialize in this effort. This approach has other benefits in that it typically results in the sections of the right of way being secured in a patchwork quilt fashion rather than successively. This provides the owner the opportunity to adjust the route should there be an issue with either a right of way or a permit. Owners usually incentivize the contracted right of way firms based on the cost efficiency with which they secure the right of way – with bonuses for less cost.

In this particular project, however, there was a twist. The owner had contracts for the use of the fiber optic line but those contracts would expire if the line was not operational by the specified deadline. If the project were not completed on time, then the contracts would expire and, unless they could be replaced, the fiber optic would remain "dark".

The project was a disaster. The contractor had a lot of productivity problems. There were permitting and environmental issues. And a few stubborn land owners held out for large sums of money for their rights of way. The project did not finish on time and the fiber optic line remained dark. I am not sure how much the owner ultimately lost but I am guessing it was at least in the tens of millions of dollars.

But guess what? That right of way contractor could proudly demonstrate how cost efficient they were in securing the right of way. And they were. Only that was part of the problem. The patchwork quilt of secured rights of way combined with the need to execute rapidly to meet the deadline meant that the owner was forced to start work on sections with secured right of way and have the contractor jump from section to section. In addition, it made those hold-out sections even more valuable because the more a line is completed, the less option there is to change the route. So, the right of way contractor maximized their bonuses based on the contract that the owner gave them. But the project failed miserably. The agenda of the right of way contractor was different from the agenda of the owner. And it was set up to be that way.

We can easily see how the same issue arises in a traditional design-bid-build project in which the owner hires a designer (architect or engineer) to design a project and then bids it out. The winning bidder is the builder (general contractor). Because of the way this process works and the various parties are compensated, they have different agendas from day 1.

- The owner typically wants the best project they can get for the money they have to spend by the deadline of when they need the project.

TRADITIONAL DESIGN-BID-BUILD RELATIONSHIP

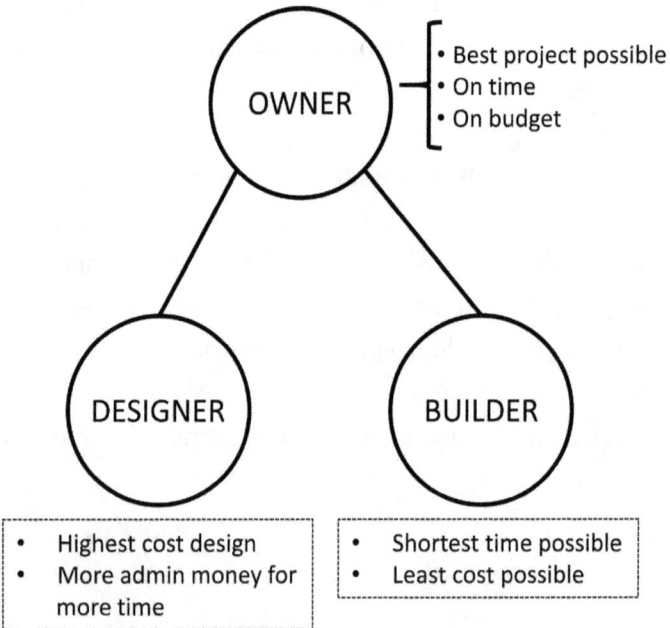

```
                    ┌─ • Best project possible
        OWNER      ─┤  • On time
                    └─ • On budget


    DESIGNER              BUILDER
```

| • Highest cost design • More admin money for more time | • Shortest time possible • Least cost possible |

- The designer gets paid as a percent plus usually gets paid for consulting during the construction phase of the project (construction administration). Therefore, if they talk the owner into a larger project (budget-wise) then they make more money and if the project schedule is extended then they are paid more for construction administration.

- The builder is the low bidder. Assuming that their bid was a good one, they make their money by getting off the project as quickly as possible with the least cost possible. If the bid was bad (i.e. they realize later they underestimated costs) then they will only make money by pursuing change orders to the contract.

In addition to these financial incentives, the designer, while ostensibly owing a responsibility to owner, is also incentivized for liability reasons to protect themselves in a case of design errors or omissions.

One project, a municipal wastewater treatment plant (WWTP), exemplified these problems. In this project, the owner needed significant renovations in order to comply with new regulations. The owner and the architecture/engineering firm worked together to design these renovations to meet the expanded needs of the municipality and increasing regulatory pressure.

The cost estimates for the original design were higher than the owner's budget so a portion of the renovation work was deleted in order to satisfy the budget. In addition, the project was left with minimal time to meet the regulatory deadline.

During the course of the project, several problems arose including a discrepancy in the design specifications for a specific component valve and a major design flaw that resulted in the purchase of specified equipment that could not perform as needed. Throughout the project, the owner repeatedly refused to recognize that these problems rested with the design and tried to push the costs to the contractor. The engineer attempted to cover up their own liability and worked with the owner to blame the contractor. The project was significantly late, and one critical piece of specified equipment worked as specified. The whole mess resulted in a lengthy litigation and millions more in costs, final settlements, and regulatory fines. The initial equipment issue could have been resolved for about $100,000. The problem with the incorrectly specified equipment was more complex but could probably have been set aside so that the main system could be completed before the regulatory deadline.

The lack of a shared agenda can be a project killer. In systems thinking, the idea of a shared agenda is called PURPOSE and will be addressed further in Part 3 – Projects as Social Systems. But, as you can see, this is not always the result of poor motives. Sometimes it is built into the very fabric of how the project is set up. In addition to this problem, there is a further issue when the project is built upon flawed operating assumptions.

6. Flawed Operating Assumptions

Projects usually include implied or hidden operating assumptions that are false. Operating assumptions are "statements" that must be true in order for the actions, structure, or inactions of the project team to make sense. A simple example at the individual level can illustrate this concept. Let us imagine that you meet me on the street. We shake hands and speak. You notice that I am not carrying an umbrella or wearing a rain coat. The obvious assumption that I have made that day is that it is not going to rain. Of course, I might just not care whether I get wet. But a reasonable assumption would be that I assumed there would be no rain. But, if you were to ask me whether or not it could rain, I would have to reply that it is possible even though I didn't expect it. But I am operating on the assumption that it will not rain. Even if I did not actually think about it ahead of time.

We do this a lot. We cannot check everything, and uncertainties require us to act on assumptions. Problems happen when those assumptions have major consequences for our project and especially when we build them into our project without even thinking about them.

A key characteristic of these hidden assumptions is their deniability. Project members would typically deny holding the assumptions if asked. But, if they do not hold them, then their actions or inactions do not make sense. The question becomes, "if they do not accept assumption 'X', then why are they doing what they are doing" or "why are they not doing 'Y'?"

Because the assumptions are hidden, it is the inactions, or omissions that are the most revealing. It is not so much what the project team is doing, but what it is not doing. It is not so much what is built into the project system as what is not built into it.

Categories of Assumptions

At least two major categories of assumptions can be hidden in a project. They are:

- **Management versus Technical:** Many assumptions involve the management of the project or even the establishment of the project to begin with. But many technical ones are made that can influence the course of a project. These include feasibility, site conditions, operating parameters, etc. They may be overriding such as the use of a specific engineering formula that only works within certain boundary conditions or they may be site-specific such as "the groundwater table at this site fluctuates between 150 and 156 feet above sea level at this location" or "the compressive strength of the soil at this site will be 2500 psi".

- **Internal versus External:** The source of the assumption may come from inside the project team or it may be imposed from the outside (higher management, clients, regulatory agencies, etc.).

In addition to these categories of assumptions, there are four assumptions that show up across different projects.

Four Common Assumptions

Four common assumptions are:

1. That the project team will remain the same for the life of the project.
2. That the project will finish on time and within budget.

3. That no intervening circumstances will stall this project (force majeure).
4. That the parts of the system share the same goals and agenda.

For example, if one were to ask a project team at the beginning of a four-year project if they will all be working on the project for the whole four years, most would reasonably answer that some of them would not. But what is built into the project system to enable it to capture the knowledge, record the decisions, and ensure project continuity when key people end up leaving? Often there is very little. This omission reveals that a team has an operating assumption as to continuity of personnel. In one project valued at several hundred million dollars, a large design-build firm went through four project managers in three years. The project experienced numerous problems and was litigated. This organization was at a distinct disadvantage in later negotiations revolving around the project schedule. Poor records and the dramatic change in personnel made it impossible to determine why certain decisions were made, when they were made, and whether or not the client had agreed to the decisions.

Similarly, most experienced project managers will say that they realize that the project might not finish on time and within budget but often there is very little built-in to the project to handle this possibility. This shows up in the ways progress is tracked, progress payments are structured, incentives and penalties are designed, risk is allocated, and the lack of effective dispute resolution techniques.

Coupled with this assumption is an even deeper one that the project MUST be completed by a certain date or at a certain amount. This ignores the fact that the schedules and budgets that drive project decisions are sometimes arbitrary and were developed and approved when the project was barely a concept. Does the project really have to finish by July 1? If so, at what cost? Many projects are accelerated for deadlines that are more or less arbitrary or without proper thought given to the cost of accelerating versus just extending the project.

Project budgets are sometimes similarly flawed. In one case, a public entity forced the architecture/engineering firm to cut 20% of the costs out of its design in order to meet the budget. During the course of the project, change orders reinstated most of these cuts and the owner ended up paying a premium and delaying the job. Faulty operating assumptions cost the owner a significant amount of money and time.

One interesting assumption involves the concept of *force majeure*. Project teams often operate on the assumption that no intervening circumstances will stall or stop this project. If the project team members were asked if they believed this, they might say "no" and point to the standard *force majeure* clause in their contract. But if they were to really think through this assumption, they might realize that were some things to be delayed, the standard clause would work against project success rather than for it. In one case, an owner was faced with a *force majeure* situation that would stall the project for six months. This construction project required a highly-specialized team of personnel that had been assembled from around the world. The owner had the standard *force majeure* clause in the contract and did not have to pay for the cost of the event to the contractor. Fortunately, the owner's attorney challenged this assumption and the owner developed a plan to pay for the key specialists to remain during the stalled time. If the owner had allowed the team to scatter, it is likely that they would not have been back in six months and the project would have suffered irreparable harm.

Another major assumption common to project systems is that everyone on the team has the same agenda. The previous chapter discussed the ways in which this assumption might be flawed, leading to adverse consequences.

7. Project Complexity

If many projects were to have a social media status, they would have to report "It's complicated." Projects are often complicated or complex. Here I am using the more common meaning of "complexity" rather than the scientific definition.

com·plex /adj.
1. composed of many interconnected parts;
compound; composite: a complex highway
system.
2. characterized by a very complicated or
involved arrangement of parts, units, etc.:
complex machinery.
3. so complicated or intricate as to be hard to
understand or deal with: a complex problem.

(dictionary.reference.com)

If we apply these definitions, we see that a more complex project has more interconnected parts, a complicated arrangement of those parts, or aspects that are difficult to understand or deal with. Clearly, complexity in this sense is not merely a function of the price of the project. Two projects that are approximately the same in terms of dollar value might differ in levels of complexity.

Imagine a road project on a straight flat piece of ground 500 miles long. The road will be straight and flat for 500 miles with no bridges, towns, etc. One team could start at one end and continue all the way to the other. Even though this project might cost a significant amount of money and thus be a "big" project, it is not necessarily complex. If the cost per lane mile is $3-4 million then a 2-lane highway would be a $3-4 billion project. Compare this to a 3 billion power plant which will include a large number of different processes which must work together to operate the completed plant. Even though the projects have the same dollar value, they differ in the complexity of what is being constructed.

Organizational interconnections might even be more important than the physical interconnections of the system being created. If we model a project organization as a network with nodes and interconnections we can see that as the number of parts (or nodes) increases, the number of possible interconnections increases quadratically. A network with only two nodes only has one interconnection whereas one with three nodes yields three interconnections. Five nodes have ten and six nodes have fifteen. The actual formula is $C = (n^2 - n)/2$. This becomes really interesting when the number of nodes increases significantly. Nine nodes yield 36 interconnections whereas 90 nodes would have 4005 interconnections. Adding just five more nodes to 95 would yield 4460 (a gain of 460 interconnections).

I am sure that at this point you are objecting: But are all of those possible interconnections real? Of course not. But there are undoubtedly more than one might realize at first glance. Possible interactions include both direct interactions and indirect interactions. Direct interactions might include such things as contracts, invoices, reporting, corre-spondence, work supervision and coordination, and litigations while indirect interactions can include interference or competition (for resources, labor, or space) or even intentional sabotage. You can probably think of a few additional ways in which the stakeholders in your project might be interconnected - even if not readily apparent at first glance.

Categories of Complexity

Beyond the inherent complexity generated by the number of nodes or stakeholders in the project, there are three categories of organizational complexity that apply to projects:

1. **Technical complexity** focuses mostly on what the project is trying to accomplish, the software being implemented, the facility being constructed, etc. The types of issues impacting technical complexity include the status of the technology (first of its kind, routine, etc.), the mix of technologies being implemented (combining legacy systems with new software for example), and the experience of the stakeholders with what is being done (how many new hospitals has this team actually built?). Technical complexity can impact almost any type of project.

2. **Management complexity** focuses on human or stakeholder issues and might include the sheer number of players involved, the organizational structure(s) in place, risk sharing amongst the parties, relative experience levels amongst stakeholders, and even the personalities of the individuals

involved and the cultures of their organizations.

3. **Environmental complexity** does not refer to the great outdoors but to the environment in which the project takes place. It includes factors such as political/ legal/ regulatory, community relations, financial/ economic conditions, and labor (unions, the availability of qualified people, etc.)

Other drivers for complexity include diversity, interdependence, ambiguity, and change.

Impacts of Complexity

Complexity can impact a project in a variety of ways but two of the biggest issues that arise are:

- Complex systems are inherently **unpredictable** which means that the potential for decisions or actions to have unintended consequences is high.
- Small changes in complex systems can have large results. The concept of tipping points, common to physical and other systems, illustrates this point.

Examples

Two examples illustrate different ways in which projects can be complex. In the first project, a large power plant, the owner made many early decisions that added to the project's complexity. One of the decisions was to attempt to control costs by buying most things (labor, material, equipment) themselves. So, rather than relying on an electrical contractor to supply its own labor and materials (conduit, wire, etc.), the owner decided it could save money by cutting out the middleman.

The owner had successfully done a series of smaller "cookie-cutter" projects this way and thought they could extrapolate this approach to the new project. But the new project was an order of magnitude larger and was also going to incorporate first of its kind technology at a commercial scale. This project quickly grew in complexity in part due to these factors and it is easy to see why. Technical complexity combined with organizational/ management complexity contributed to massive budget overruns and delays. At one point, this project had materials, labor, and equipment from over 180 vendors and subcontractors purchased directly by the owner. In our calculation of theoretical interconnections between nodes – this would indicate 16,2000 possible interconnections. And it showed even in the difficulties of day-to-day coordination. For example, there were multiple electrical contractors responsible for performing different aspects of the project. At some points, they were actually competing for conduit when the owner had not purchased enough for everybody and it was given out on a first-come-first-serve basis with no regard for project work priorities. This project experienced massive cost overruns and extensive schedule delays.

Boston's "Big Dig" is a famously disastrous project in terms of budget and schedule. One part of this project exemplified technical complexity in the way it combined low tech and high tech in a long-term project. Underground roads require an immense network of various types of controls (twenty-two systems in total including HVAC, fire, safety cameras, and alarm systems). The relatively high-tech control systems and their software and hardware requirements were tied into the low-tech aspects of the project from both a scheduling standpoint as well as from the need for certain physical tunnels and conduits to be completed before the control wiring could be placed. The overall project duration was extended by years. This had two unexpected consequences. First, the schedule required the controls contractor to continue to rush to meet deadlines that, when met, were rendered meaningless by the fact that the physical work (i.e. the tunnels and the conduit) were not complete. This resulted in numerous start-stop delays and the termination and replacement of the original contractor.

The second unexpected consequence was that this was all happening during a time of rapid technological progress on all fronts. The nineties and early 2000's saw rapid increases in data processing speeds, the invention of the world-wide web, video gaming and new expectations for user interfaces, Microsoft Windows, etc. The controls system was initially designed using early nineties technology and expectations but would not be completed until well into this revolution. The system architecture was designed around sub-systems capabilities that changed rapidly over time and equipment that was rendered obsolete before the system could even be put in place. This resulted in a huge clash between software and hardware as well as user expectations and actual contractual responsibilities. In fact, in hindsight, much of this could have been avoided using an approach in which the physical low-tech work would be done first and then the high-tech controls work would be designed and implemented in a fairly rapid manner with no physical impediments and with built-in plans for technological obsolescence.

An approach to project management that accounts for possible complexity should assist you in first limiting complexity wherever possible. Second, where it is not possible to limit complexity, the approach should provide built in mechanisms for ongoing learning and adaptation as the project progresses including identifying possible issues related to complexity and monitoring those issues to adapt as necessary.

In addition to complexity, projects face many other risks. The next chapter describes external risks and the implications of these potential problems.

8. External Risks

Beyond the challenges that can be baked into the project itself, projects face many external threats or challenges from a variety of sources. I will spend more time discussing risks and risk management in later chapters but want to mention them in this section to further flesh out the types of challenges your project might face.

Some common external risks can be grouped into three categories:

- Regulatory/ Legal/ Political
- Financial/ Economic
- Natural and Man-made Disasters

Regulatory/ Legal/ Political Risks

Regulatory and legal risks to your project might include anything from not receiving the approvals necessary for the project to not getting the sign-off by building code inspectors at the end. The following can kill or seriously impact your project: changing regulations related to the type of facility you are building; political pressure brought to bear on government officials to modify or halt your project; and changes in zoning or unwillingness to approve zoning exceptions. If you are in an industry where projects are highly regulated (power, pipeline, etc.), the cooperation of the regulators and a thorough understanding of the regulatory process is essential.

Financial/ Economic Risks

Financial and economic risks in this case refer to those larger financial or economic events that could impact your project from the outside:

- Your ability to get financing for the project due to availability of credit in the financial market.
- The solvency of the bank or banks financing your project.
- The impact to your bottom line of carrying a project of extended duration.

- The effects the project might have on your current business.
- Changes in pricing for global commodities (e.g. what impact does a rise in copper prices have on your project if it includes a lot of electrical wiring?).
- Shortages of labor or the specific skill sets you need or general labor unrest.
- Shortages of materials either regionally due to a large number of projects or globally (e.g. we have seen both steel and concrete shortages in the past few decades).

Any economic or financial events that could impact your organization could impact your project. This is especially true if your project lasts over several years and you do not have a magical crystal ball to see what will happen. Of course, if you do find such a crystal ball, you can retire from project management to trade commodities.

Natural and Man-made Disasters

These risks include the obvious threats such as earthquakes, floods, tsunamis, mudslides, forest fires, tornadoes, and hurricanes. Keep in mind that these risks do NOT have to happen at the site where you are building in order to impact your project. They could happen to a supplier of key equipment or materials. Or even in transit. I was once involved in a project in which a vital piece of equipment fell off of a ship in a storm in the Pacific. Lions, and tigers, and bears, oh my!

9. Project Challenges Self-Assessment

In this Part, I described several types and categories of challenges faced by projects in the real world along with providing examples and explaining the implications. The purpose of this chapter is to summarize these challenges with a list of questions that you should ask yourself (or maybe your team) about your project.

As you think about your project, ask yourself the following questions:

1. Are all of your team members operating with the same goals?
2. Can any of your team members win even if the project loses?
3. What unintended consequences could be caused by your project?

4. What would be the consequences to your organization of a total failure to meet this project's objectives? Or a partial failure to meet one or more of the cost, schedule, quality, operational, branding, and inspirational objectives?

5. What critical assumptions have you built into your project?

6. What hidden assumptions are there that you did not realize?

7. Have all key parts of your project system had input into assumptions, contingency planning, etc.?

8. Do you know how you will quickly validate those assumptions or how you will detect false assumptions?

9. Have you created a detailed set of contingency plans for this project?

10. Do your contingencies include at least one from each of the external risk categories?

Part 3
Projects as
Social Systems

*The more efficient you are at doing the
wrong thing, the wronger you become.
It is much better to do the right thing
wronger than the wrong thing righter.
If you do the right thing wrong and
correct it, you get better.*
--- Russell Ackoff

Part 3 – Projects as Social Systems

10. What is Systems Thinking?

Systems thinking is a view of the world that focuses on the whole rather than just the parts, the forest rather than the trees. Its opposite view, reductionism, rests on the idea that you can best learn about anything by breaking it down into ever smaller parts and trying to understand each of the parts and then trying to assemble the understanding of the parts into an understanding of the whole. Reductionism has been a staple of science for most of the past 500 years.

The ancient Greek philosopher, Democritus, coined the term "atom" to hypothesize about nature's elemental building blocks. But it took Sir Isaac Newton to popularize a view of the universe as a set of billiard balls functioning in a predictable manner based upon strict cause and effect. The combined atomistic-mechanistic viewpoint became the dominant scientific paradigm of the last 500 years. It became dominant because of its successes. It led to ever greater discoveries as it pushed scientists to break nature into ever smaller parts for study and experimentation. In chemistry and physics, this led to particle physics and the drive to break down matter into smaller and smaller bits. In biology, this approach led to increasingly detailed taxonomies, the study of biochemistry, the discovery of DNA, and the field of genetics.

The world of ideas always links to the world of action and these same views and approaches increasingly found expression in society. Through Descartes, Hobbes, and Locke, atomism found its way into the paradigm of the new American Republic at the same time that mechanistic thinking was working its way into industry. In the middle of the 20th century, when these ideas were seeing their greatest successes and widest applications, and, arguably their greatest failures as well, science was beginning the slow process of moving to a new paradigm due to the increasingly obvious problems encountered in the old paradigm.

Quantum mechanics was reporting that the material world might be uncertain and unpredictable. Later, biologists such as Ludwig Von Bertalanffy began to recognize that biologists could literally be missing the forest by studying the trees. Bertalanffy, in his seminal work on general systems science, proposed, among other things, that one could not necessarily understand the whole by studying only the parts. More recently, chaos and complexity theorists have pushed the edge of uncertainty further in an attempt to better understand the random or nonlinear aspects of nature, discovering patterns in the process.

Like the earlier atomistic-mechanistic view, the systemic view has also begun to influence the world of human interactions. In the world of business and organizations, thinkers such as Russell Ackoff, Peter Senge, Peter Checkland, and Jay Forester extended the influence of systems thinking into areas such as organizational development, cybernetics, and learning organizations. In particular, Ackoff's approach to systems thinking has been successfully applied in organizations as diverse as Fortune 500 companies, government, and non-profits.

Systems thinking, or systemics, is a view of the world that seeks to understand the whole first and then understand the parts in the context of their function in the whole system. The following table compares the basic principles of a systemic approach and its means of thinking, synthesis, with that of an atomistic-mechanistic viewpoint and its primary means of thinking, analysis.

Atomistic-Mechanistic Approach (Analysis)	Systemic Approach (Synthesis)
Focuses on breaking apart the whole into its constituent elements and then studying those elements (reductionism).	Focuses on the whole as a system and the interactions between the parts.
Success is optimization of the parts.	Success is optimization of the whole. In fact, a basic principle is that the whole **cannot** be optimized by optimizing the parts.
Emphasizes minute detail – the trees.	Emphasizes the "big picture" – the forest.
Modifies one variable at a time (the Scientific Method).	Modifies multiple variables in an experimental redesign.
Leads to a management style in which activities and tasks are the focus and are planned out in detail. Forecasted results are the key metric.	Leads to a management approach in which action is governed by the objectives and purposes of the system and its larger environment.

	Assumptions are the key metric.
Discipline oriented.	Meta-disciplinary or multi-disciplinary.
Focuses on following the plan.	Focuses on learning and adaptation to a changing environment and set of assumptions.

Systems thinking does not deny the usefulness of an analytical or reductionist approach. Instead, it seeks to place it within the proper context.

While this Part of the book might seem to be theoretical, I cannot overemphasize its importance. In my own journey, I was at a point at which my primary work consisted of analyzing projects that had performed poorly. In doing so, I began to notice patterns of problems across project types and across industries. I discovered Ackoff's approach to systems thinking for organizations. Delving into that work completely changed my understanding of projects. To understand why, it is critical to understand Ackoff's levels of systems, and, in particular, social systems.

11. Systems Thinking and Social Systems

Not all systems are created equal. Russell Ackoff's work categorizes systems in terms of purpose and includes four types: deterministic, animated, social, and ecological. In deterministic systems, neither the parts nor the whole have a purpose. Examples include machines. Any purpose that a machine has is extrinsic – it comes from the outside, from the machine's creator. Animated systems have a purpose as a whole but their parts do not have a purpose although they have functions within the whole. Animals are examples of animated systems. Social systems have purposeful parts and a purposeful whole while ecological systems have purposeful parts but no purposeful whole.

Social systems are systems involving people and purpose. Purpose makes social systems distinct from other sorts of systems. Social systems are purposeful systems containing purposeful parts and are typically contained within a larger purposeful system – either social or ecological.

Organizations are social systems. Organizations are made up of people or sub-organizations that interact with each other to create the whole system. An organization as a whole has a purpose. But each of the people or sub-organizations that comprise it also have their own purposes.

The very thing that makes social systems unique is also what makes them difficult to model effectively. Mechanistic models that assume an organization is a deterministic system or organic models that assume that an organization is an animated system may show some success but each overlook critical data in the form of purpose. The first assumes no purpose whatsoever while the second assumes that the individual parts have no purpose. Each approach may increase the efficiency of some or all of the parts but seldom increases the effectiveness of the system and is likely to actually decrease system effectiveness over time.

12. Re-Thinking the Project Mindset

Radical improvement of project performance is impossible as long as projects are approached in the same way as they have been in the past. Refinements of technique can lead, at best, to incremental gains in project performance and cannot compensate for the systemic and structural problems that plague capital projects.

Dealing with systemic and structural problems requires systems thinking. Systems thinking suggests that part of the reason that projects fail can be found in the way that projects are defined. Mindset begins with definition. This is not to say that the failure is merely one of semantics but that the way projects are defined – as a set of tasks or activities – encourages a viewpoint that is not necessarily conducive to project success. An activities-based viewpoint of the project encourages project owners to forget the most significant aspects of any project – the people and organizations making up the project and their interactions and ability or inability to react to changes during the project.

The current, commonly used definitions of "project" are a problem. They focus us toward the parts of the system and guide us in trying to break down projects into a larger number of smaller parts in the hope that we can better manage them. By viewing a project as a set of tasks, we avoid the real issues of project management which are (or at least should be) largely about how to create an effective, temporary organization to accomplish an important purpose with the resources we have available.

Project management techniques focus on the symptoms rather than on disease. They help you keep score but do not help you score points. They push the focus away from the most important success factors which are people and interaction related.

A systems approach starts with a view of projects as social systems rather than as a collection of tasks, or an endeavor. Social systems are different from other types of systems in that the system as a whole (the organization) is purposeful and the parts of the system (either individuals or sub-organizations) are also purposeful. The system and its parts each have their own purposes. The endeavor being undertaken is the purpose of the purposeful system but it is not the system itself. A systems thinking view of project management begins with a new definition of "project" itself:

A Project is a temporary social system or organization created to accomplish a specific purpose with designated resources.

Projects are temporary organizations created to accomplish a purpose which is that specific endeavor or set of tasks. The facility or pipeline or factory or piece of infrastructure you are building is NOT the project – it is the PURPOSE of the project. This is not just a change in semantics but a change in focus and mindset with a range of implications.

First, each part in the project social system, whether an individual or organization (engineer, contractor, vendor, stakeholder), has its own purpose and acts according to its purpose. In addition, the project as a whole has a purpose. The endeavor that is the subject of earlier definitions is, itself, the purpose of the social system created to accomplish it.

Second, because the interactions do more to define the characteristics (and thus effectiveness) of the whole system, managing those interactions is of primary importance.

And third, because the future cannot be accurately predicted, the system must incorporate mechanisms for learning and adaptation.

In addition to a new definition, a new project model can further a systems thinking mindset. The next chapter (13) describes such a model. Then, Chapter 14 will further explain the implications of a systems approach.

13. A Project Systems Model

A project model as a system can help to foster this new mindset as well as to highlight several important aspects of what it means for a project to be a system. David Cleland and William King developed a model of an organization as a social system.[14] I adapted and expanded this model to better conceptualize the project as a social system with all of its complex interactions (on the next page).

If we look at this model and work our way outside from the center, then we can see the following:

- The parent organization, which is the owner of the project, is made up of a variety of functional areas and sub-organizations. These might be organized in a variety of ways but are shown here as separate functional areas. A project typically cuts across several functions and includes people, resources, and processes from each for its success.

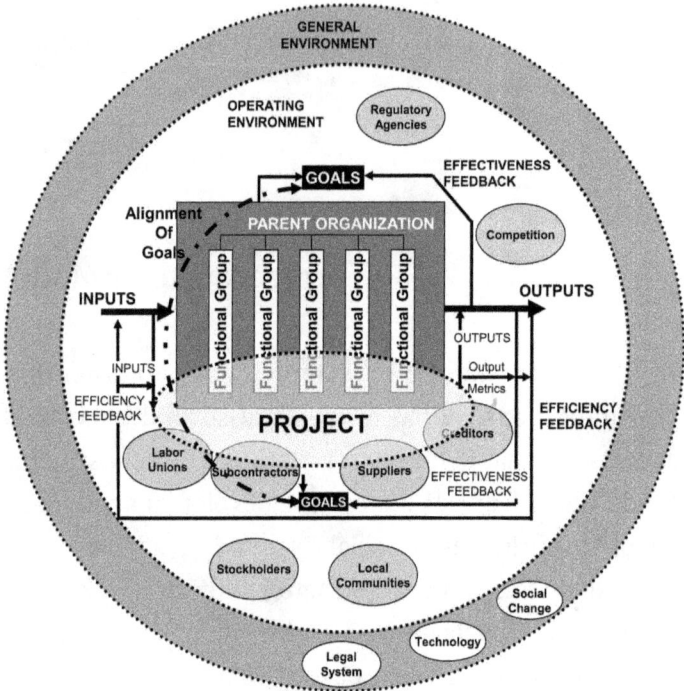

PROJECT SYSTEM MODEL

- The parent organization has inputs and outputs which include every resource and person that comes into the organization or leaves it.
- The fundamental difference between effectiveness and efficiency is that Effectiveness is a measurement of outputs vs.

goals, what you achieve versus what you wanted to achieve, whereas efficiency is a measure of how much of your inputs you have used to produce your outputs. This is an important implication to understand and will be discussed at greater length in the next chapter.

- The parent organization is surrounded by its operating environment which also may include a number of other organizations that are part of the project.

- The project has goals of its own. Those goals must be aligned to the parent organization's goals. The project also has inputs and outputs which result in its own measures of effectiveness and efficiency.

- This entire system operates in a general environment that includes a legal system, technology, and social changes – all of which can have an impact on the parent organization, the project, and its parts.

Definitions and models can help to think about what it means for a project to be a social system. But there are additional and important implications that arise from a systems approach to projects. The next chapter describes these in detail.

14. Implications of a Systems Approach

We are able to apply a systems approach when we redefine "project" from "endeavor or tasks" to a "temporary organization." A systems approach to project management has implications throughout every aspect of the project, from initial organizational design and development, contracting approach and language, involvement of key stakeholders, to the design, implementation, and purpose of project controls.

Implications of a systems approach include:

- Optimizing the whole.
- Symptoms are not causes.
- Interactions are critical.
- Effectiveness is more essential than efficiency.

- Errors of omission are worse than errors of commission.
- Assumptions rather than forecasts.
- Implementing a design approach.
- Importance of learning and adaptation.

Optimizing the Whole

A fundamental rule of systems is that you cannot optimize the whole system by optimizing the parts of the system. In fact, the opposite is often true. Take a common mechanical system for example, the automobile.

Every type of automobile is designed with a specific purpose in mind. The purpose might have a number of components such as intended functionality, intended market, planned price point, etc. But if we look at just one of these, intended functionality, it is clear that the whole automobile must be optimized toward this purpose. Every part becomes a trade-off. If we are trying to design a rugged off-road vehicle then we are not likely to put in an engine designed for a Formula One racecar. It is not enough to ask what is the best engine, transmission, suspension, body type. We must ask what is the best engine for THIS particular automobile with its particular purpose. Every choice is essentially a trade-off. This is true of most mechanical systems. Think of an army tank for example. The design of every tank faces certain trade-offs such as speed (how fast will the tank be able to move) vs protection (how much armor, and therefore weight, will it have).

The same is true of social systems. Having all the best "parts" on your team might not give you the best team. Think about a sports team. Is it better to have a team of all-stars that cannot play together or a team of good players that play well as a team? The declining success of America's Dream Team in Olympic basketball in recent years illustrates the fact that teams of good players playing well together can often beat a team of superstars that cannot play together (whether from lack of experience playing together or an unwillingness to put aside ego for team). Good parts that function well together are better than great parts that cannot interact properly. No system can be optimized as a whole through the optimization of the parts. And this includes your project as a social system. Yet the traditional project management approach to a project is to view it as a set of things (tasks, time, money, risks) to be broken down into ever smaller pieces to each be managed and optimized.

Symptoms are not Causes

Symptoms are not causes. We know this well when it comes to one system with which we are intimately familiar – our bodies. A headache is a symptom. So is an upset stomach. But the pain or upset that we feel is not what is causing the pain or upset. In fact, often, for any symptom there are a range of potential causes. A corollary of this systems principle is that, when dealing with problems, not only is the symptom not the cause but the best solution for the problem might be to intervene at a point in the system that is different from where the symptom (or even the cause) appears. So, you have a pain in your head and you do not go to see a neurosurgeon (at least not without a lot more diagnosis). More frequently, you swallow a pill that goes down your throat into your stomach. You have intervened at a point well removed from your symptom. The same principle often applies to organizations. The best point to intervene to solve a problem might not be the part of the system where the problem is found.

Ackoff often told a story about an intervention in a company that was in the business of manufacturing quality papers for stationery, art books, etc. Manufacturing was having a difficult time keeping up with the wide range of papers produced due to short runs and the reset times needed for the machinery for each run. It appeared to be a manufacturing optimization problem. Ackoff's recommendation was to dissolve the problem by changing the incentive structure for the sales team! They identified the most profitable and popular items being produced and incentivized the sales staff to sell those items more than any other. The sales force stopped selling the unprofitable items. The resulting decrease in items produced relieved the pressure on the manufacturing process. Without one change to manufacturing processes, this intervention succeeded in fixing the "manufacturing" problem in the organization. It also made the company more profitable.

Symptoms are not causes. And problems are often best solved by interventions away from the symptoms or even the cause. This is true of your body and your project organization.

Interactions are Critical

> *"To manage a system effectively, you might focus on the interactions of the parts rather than their behavior taken separately."*
> *--- Russell Ackoff*

In a system, the interactions between the parts are as important to success as the parts themselves. In a mechanical system, such as an engine, the interactions include: the timing; the friction (and lubrication to prevent friction); the interconnecting belts, tubes, and ducts; etc. If these interactions are off, the engine will fail.

In the world of project management, the interactions of the physical system being built are often the most difficult to design, estimate, track, and often cause problems later during start-up or operation. In estimation for example, estimators usually get major components right but can often have problems with the interconnections. Take a co-gen power plant, for example. Usually the major components such as the turbine generator, the heat recovery steam generator, etc. are easily estimated. There are not a lot of purchasing options and the prices are fairly easy to ascertain. What gets tricky however are the miles of wiring and conduit and piping, the terminations, the controllers, and all of the "little" items that go into making the plant operational. These items are more frequently the cause of estimate "busts". They can also cause ample headaches during start-up and commissioning when a small improperly installed connection can cause a large problem.

The same holds true for the interactions of the parts of your project social system. Failures to communicate and interact in ways that align with the success of the project will lead to project failure. Interactions are critical to project success at every level.

Effectiveness is More Essential than Efficiency

"Efficiency is doing things right;
effectiveness is doing the right things."
--- *Peter Drucker*

As highlighted by the Ackoff quote at the beginning of Part 3 as well as the Drucker quote above, it is better to do the right thing "wronger" than the wrong thing "righter". Our model of a project system in Chapter 13 illustrates the difference between effectiveness and efficiency. But it is difficult to imagine giving this concept too much emphasis. If your car is careening to the edge of a cliff, efficiency would involve covering more ground in less time and would imply that you should hit the accelerator. If we assume however, that your goal is not to die, effectiveness would involve doing anything you could to slow the car's progress and prevent it from going over the cliff. Even if it involved mechanically wrecking the car.

A fundamental implication of a systems understanding of projects is this difference between efficiency and effectiveness. Efficiency compares outputs to inputs. An efficiency mindset asks, "How much are you getting per dollar spent?" Effectiveness compares outputs to goals. An effectiveness mindset asks, "Are you accomplishing your goals?" and, "What should your goals be?" This is true for both the parent organization and the project organization. It is quite possible, and even quite common, to be efficient in doing the wrong thing. You can drive from Point A to Point B very efficiently in terms of directness, speed, fuel mileage, etc. But if Point B is not where you should be going then your efficient efforts are not effective. You are literally "going nowhere fast".

The example of the fiber optic line project given in Chapter 5 illustrates this point well. The consultant hired to secure the right of way was actually incentivized to be efficient. But given the project's purpose and the importance of the deadline to its success – this efficiency was contrary to the effectiveness of the project. Ultimately, a project has no value until somebody "buys" it at the end. Whether that means literally buying space (e.g. residential, commercial, or retail development projects), buying the products that will be produced (e.g. manufacturing, power, oil & gas), or buying the service that the project makes possible (e.g. fiber optic communications or medical services at a hospital).

Ideally of course, one should be both effective and efficient. One should be heading toward one's goals in as efficient a manner as possible. But spending time focusing on efficiency might kill your project – if you have not first spent time ensuring effectiveness.

Omissions are Worse than Commissions

In Catholic theology, there is a two-pronged concept of sinning. It is the idea that you can sin in what you did as well as in what you failed to do that you should have done. While we are not concerned with sins here, systems thinking brings an analogous concept – errors of commission and errors of omission.

Errors of commission include things that you did as an organization that were not well done or were wrong for the intended purpose. The key here is that you DID them. You committed the acts.

Errors of omission involve things that you SHOULD have done but did not do. You should have taken the road less traveled but you did not.

Omissions are generally worse than commissions. Companies have gone bust because they did not react to changes in the market or because they did not consider some aspect of their product that later proved to be detrimental to sales.

Of course, a big omission in organizations (whether permanent or project) is to fail to consider the systems aspects of the organization, the omission of systems thinking altogether.

Assumptions Rather than Forecasts

Modern management is built largely around a forecasting mindset. Yet we are not generally good at forecasting. We are not omniscient. If I am wrong, and you are good at forecasting then go buy the winning lottery ticket tonight and pass this book on to somebody who needs it. But I am not. We forecast and we forecast but we often get them wrong. But the forecasting approach is built into the way management is done and infects decision-making, approvals, tracking and monitoring, rewards and incentives, and evaluations of success or failure.

> *"The future is better dealt with using*
> *assumptions than forecasts."*
> *--- Russell Ackoff*

In systems thinking, assumptions are more important than forecasts. Some of the same analytical tools might be used. However, viewing the result as a working assumption rather than a forecasted answer changes the mindset significantly. When forecasts guide the management process, the focus is to try to make the forecast come true. When assumptions guide the process, the focus is to try to validate or invalidate the assumption as quickly as possible.

I would propose that this is not merely semantics. Think about these two approaches expressed in terms of a project description:

A. Our project budget is $20 million. We are building a facility that has x, y, and z features and it will be done and ready for use in 18 months.

B. We need a facility with x, y, and z features. The business case tells us that this facility will help us most if it can be completed in 18 months and our initial assumption after discussions with the contractor are that this is feasible. In addition, our working assumption about cost (also based on our business case/justification) is that this project can be completed for $20 million. We intend to further validate these assumptions also at the 90% phase and make any decisions needed at that time (go, no go, modification, reconsideration of the business case, etc.).

Which of these approaches is more likely to lead to a project that ultimately is late and costs 10% more with an unhappy board of directors who didn't know until two-thirds of the budget was expended that there was a problem? In my experience analyzing dozens of failed projects, option A is more likely to quickly result in a feverish attempt to make budget and schedule without ever considering whether it was feasible or not or needed to be adjusted. An assumption approach to project management will radically change the way you think about projcts, approvals, and project controls. It will be an important part of Chapter 22 – Learning and Adaptation – and Chapter 25 – Re-thinking Project Controls.

Implementing a Design Approach

Systems thinking focuses on dissolving problems rather than solving them. It does this by designing the problems out of systems rather than trying to solve them reactively. Do not play "whack a mole". Do not leave holes for the moles to pop up in the first place.

Ackoff's matchbook story illustrates this principle well. A manufacturer of the matchbooks that you typically receive for free at places that sell cigarettes had a problem. Every year, an almost predictable number of people would open a matchbook, take out a match, strike the striker pad located at the bottom of the front of the matchbook and proceed to light the rest of the matches on fire by accident – resulting in a burn. This would often result in a lawsuit. Equating symptoms and

causes and wanting to prevent lawsuits, the company turned to its legal department for a solution to the lawsuit problem. The legal department suggested the type of disclaimer/ instructions that have become common on all sorts of projects due to excessive litigation. The warning, right at the bottom of the flap, said "CLOSE COVER BEFORE STRIKING".

It turns out that this warning made very little impact on the annual number of burnt hand lawsuits. Maybe that is because smoking is so readily combined with judgement-impairing activities like drinking alcohol. Maybe not. Either way, this problem was still unresolved until a young man told them he could solve their problem for a fee and that the solution would cost no more to manufacture. Once they agreed to the fee, only payable if he gave them a solution that would work, they asked, "What is the solution?".

He turned to the president of the company and said, "Put the striking pad on the back of the matchbook." With that simple change to the design, the company made it almost impossible to accidently ignite the entire book of matches. It was designing the problem out of the product rather than trying to "solve" the problem. Federal safety legislation in 1973 actually mandated this re-design to a product that, otherwise, had barely changed in almost a century.

A design approach to project management means that you design your temporary organization rather than just "letting it happen" or doing it the way it has always been done. You do this up-front, employing the principles of systems thinking, because every decision you make impacts downstream cost. The next part of this book, Part 4, focuses on designing project success.

Part 4
Designing
Project Success

Well begun is half done.

--- Aristotle

Part 4 – Designing Project Success

15. Design Principles

Common definitions of "project" focus our attention on the tasks or the endeavor to be completed. And as engineers and project managers, we tend to be comfortable with that focus. The team however, is the most important aspect of any project. A project is, more than anything else, a temporary organization created for a specific purpose, i.e. a social system.

I have been thinking of projects as social systems and evaluating the applicability of systems thinking to project management for over fifteen years and have been involved in dozens of projects across a range of industries. A systems approach provides a framework for understanding why projects succeed or fail. Through this lens, I identified what I think are the seven design principles necessary to incorporate the implications of systems thinking discussed in the previous Part. I believe that a failure to incorporate these design principles will lead to project failures in one or more ways. However, these are not a description of THE way to organize your project. They are principles that should be incorporated when you **design your project organization** and plan your execution. Every project's purpose and parts (stakeholders) are different. The art is to be able to apply these principles, as well as the tools described later in Part 5, in your unique situation to come up with success as you defined it when you set out on your project adventure.

The seven design principles to be included are:

1. Purpose creation.
2. Purpose alignment.
3. Coordinated effort.
4. Effective communication.
5. Detailed planning.
6. Effective and efficient execution.
7. Learning and adaptation.

These design principles constitute the next seven chapters. It is not a coincidence that the first two focus on purpose. It also should not surprise you that these seven principles overlap and are inter-connected. After all, that is only fitting in a set of principles derived from systems thinking.

16. Purpose Creation

What is your project's purpose? We have already covered how important purpose is to a social system and, thus, to your project and will discuss it again as part of the next chapter. But what is "purpose" and how do you get it and define it?

"Purpose", as commonly used, indicates the reason why you are doing something. The purpose is the objective, the goal, the desired result. So, in the case of a project as social system, the Purpose is that which you are building. It must align with the organization's purpose or goals as well. So, let us start there.

Why are you doing the Project?

Why is your organization undertaking a project in the first place? What is the business reason or justification for spending resources and what do you hope to gain? And of course, each cause has another cause before it so this business reason should relate to your organization's overall purpose or reason for being. Understanding that is beyond the scope of this book but, arguably, if you do not have a clearly designed purpose (vision, mission, goal) for your organization then any resources spent are wasted and you are, like the quote earlier from *Alice in Wonderland*, going nowhere.

Let us assume for a moment that you are a hospital. Your hospital's overall purpose might be:

> *To serve our community by providing high quality healthcare and creating enough of a surplus (for a non-profit) or profit to grow in number served, types of services offered, and quality of services.*

Why might this hospital undertake a project? To modernize its facilities? To expand them in order to accommodate more patients? To provide services that were not offered before in a new way? Maybe a new outpatient surgery center or the addition of a trauma center? The board of directors of this organization might have any number of reasons or combinations of reasons for undertaking a project. Or even several projects. In fact, there might be more possible projects than there are resources. It is not enough to clearly identify the "why" but it is also important to identify and clearly understand the "why not" that went with various other alternatives.

The goal of this step of the process is to clearly answer the following questions:

0. What is the overall purpose of this organization (this should already be known of course which is why I made it number zero)?
1. What is the purpose for undertaking a project?
    a. What problem does it solve or what opportunity will it create?
    b. How does it fulfill the organization's overall purpose?
2. What alternatives were decided against and why?
3. What are the desired benefits to be achieved by accomplishing this project? And how narrow was the margin between this choice and the alternatives?
4. What are the resources (money, time, team members) that are available to accomplish this purpose?

Clearly, not every purpose can be accomplished and not every project should be attempted. At this point, when you are creating the purpose, there are already some assumptions being made about costs, benefits, timing, etc. As discussed in the previous Part, assumptions are different than forecasts. And any assumptions at this stage should be based on the best information available and should be completely transparent to all of the decision makers. There should also be scheduled various points at which the project team will need to try to validate (or invalidate) these assumptions and those points should be established ahead of time with clear reporting and even reconsideration of the decision if needed. Far too many projects proceed on the assumption that it is possible to do X for $Y in Z days when, in reality, one or more of those metrics is extremely difficult or impossible to achieve. As discussed before, framing these as operating assumptions rather than forecasts, and doing so transparently should help to avoid the mindset that starts with a forecast and tries to make it true regardless of the facts. If the hole is round then do not hammer in a square peg.

What does Purpose look like?

When developing your project's purpose, keep in mind that it should incorporate the critical assumptions as well as how it fulfills the purpose of your parent organization. So, a project for the above hospital system might have an outlined purpose as follows:

Our hospital, in coordination with ABC Oncology Partners and through our project team will design, construct and open a new, state of the art, cancer treatment center by May 1, 2020 at a cost of no more than $75 million. When completed, this project will make our hospital the leading cancer treatment hospital in the tri-state area allowing us to treat an additional 25% oncology patients yearly and providing an increase in positive outcomes - saving more lives and bringing greater health to our region.

In addition, the purpose statement should have an accompanying document that shows the analysis of alternatives and the business case/justification for this project as well as referencing the two major assumptions made here (cost and timing) and what information formed the basis for those assumptions. It should also specify future decision points where those assumptions will be re-examined (some project management approaches have similar decision points referred to as stage-gates).

Note that one of the tools included in Part 5, idealized design, can be an effective tool for determining both the organization's and the project's purposes.

17. Purpose Alignment

Creating a united front, operating in a win-win environment, rallying around the flag, rowing in the same direction, playing from the same sheet of music... If it seems as though I'm exhausting metaphors – good. I want you to understand that this could well be the single most important aspect of project design. Alignment of purpose is arguably the single most important design principle. A project divided against itself will fail just as surely as a house divided against itself will fall.

Alignment essentially means that each component of the project social system – whether individual or organization, owner or contractor, engineer or vendor, not only has a purpose but shares the same purpose or at least compatible purposes. A project that can fail for the owner and still be successful for the contractor or the engineer will almost always fail. Shared purpose does not have to be soft and "touchy-feely".

Shared purpose shows itself in many "real" aspects of the project including:

- Incentives including obvious ones such as shared savings as well as a lack of dis-incentives such as a pricing scheme that encourages behavior contrary to overall project success.
- Mission statements.
- Project charters.
- Contracting strategy and language (at all levels).
- Early involvement of key players.
- Participative team selection process.
- Innovative project structures and organizational designs.

Misalignment also shows itself in many different ways. As discussed in Chapter 5 in the discussion of competing agendas, think of the traditional design – bid – build style of approach to contracting. Often, this approach violates the principle of alignment in almost every way. The contractor can succeed by providing lower quality and by getting off the project as quickly as possible to meet the bid estimate. The engineer gets paid a percentage and can actually make more money if the project costs more. Players critical to the success of the project are not brought into the team until it is too late to make best use of their insights. The owner wants the best quality possible for its budget. And yet, this approach incentivizes each party to act contrary to the interests of the others. While this is an egregious example, many projects contain both subtle, and not so subtle, examples of misalignments in purposes among the parties. To prevent this, the project team must design alignment into its contracting approach, organizational design, and systems. Likewise, it must root out misalignment at every opportunity.

In order to be successfully aligned, Purpose must be:

- **Communicated:** The purpose must be clearly defined, explicitly described, and transparent both in terms of intent and assumptions.
- **Understood:** Everyone on the team must understand the purpose and how it applies to their own role in the project. There is an old saying about playing "on the same sheet of music". But that is actually a simplification. In an orchestra, for example, the musicians playing each type of instrument actually have different sheets of music focused on the roles

and abilities of their instrument. But all of these different sheets of music, at their core, represent the same musical piece that the orchestra is playing.

- **Agreed:** There must be buy-in amongst the various parts of the social system. The purpose needs to permeate the entire system and be owned and assimilated by the various team members and sub-organizations.

- **Reinforced:** Finally, the purpose should be reinforced through incentives/ disincentives, repetition, decisions, and reviews/ tracking.

In construction, contracts govern almost every relationship between team members who are not part of the same organization. Typically, contracts were created over time by what I call accretion. Accretion occurs every time a lawyer becomes familiar with a specific project problem and tries to write contract language to deal with that problem in the future. Usually this language tries to resolve the problem by legal means rather than by a systems approach designed to modify the organization to prevent the problem from occurring. Because of this, an essential part of any purpose alignment process will be to involve lawyers who can think "outside the box" and craft legal instruments that align the purposes of the team members and the purpose of the project.

Rigorously rooting out misalignment

Any misalignments need to be rigorously rooted out and eliminated. Elimination might be revision of policies or incentives or it could involve the removal and replacement of a team member who is not willing to buy-in and act in the best interests of the project.

Purpose maps can be a useful tool for testing a project for misalignment. The purpose map, looking similar to an influence diagram or even a "mind map", shows the various parts of the system and their relationships to each other. It also identifies the key documents that govern those relationships as well as the important common interactions between the parts. Once completed, the parts and the interactions can be tested by looking at sample documents and through discussions with personnel to identify problems in areas such as:

- Incentives.
- Contracts.
- Conflicts that might be simmering in plain view or below the surface.
- Pressures within stakeholder organizations that might lead to competing agendas.

- Capacity or lack of capacity (financial or other resources). Nothing can change an agenda faster than the realization that the organization might suffer a financial loss if the purpose is realized.

Misalignment of purpose can be intentional as when a party chooses not to make the project's purpose its own. It can also be unintentional and result from circumstances or mistakes that arise during the project even though the parties involved intended to achieve the purpose. Unfortunately, as projects have been done in the past, misalignments are often *nonintentional.* A nonintentional misalignment occurs when the parties to the project have never considered this issue at all. It is neither intentional nor unintentional but lacks intention altogether.

What does Aligned Purpose look like?

Every project will and should be different. However, there are various project formats that have been implemented in the past that point the way toward what a project operating with an aligned purpose could look like. Some of these have even been proposed due to realizations of the flaws in traditional project organizations but have not gone far enough in modifying the organization or, where successful, have been so *nonintentionally* from a systems perspective.

These examples include:

- Partnering.
- Project companies.
- Skunkworks.
- Lean Construction and Integrated Project Delivery.

Partnering is a method that involves creating a project charter up front and getting the project team members to agree to the charter. It is an attempt to solve the types of problems that I have described in this book. However, it usually does not go far enough. Most often, the underlying contractual structures of the project are not changed much and the competing agendas are still there but being glossed over.

The US Army Corps of Engineers has been a huge proponent of project partnering over the years. Years ago, I attended a presentation on partnering at a Corps conference. The presenters included a partnering facilitator and a Corps project manager. One of the slides showed satisfaction with project partnering from the perspectives of project managers from both the Corps and the contractors. It was admittedly non-scientific and only covered 50-60 projects in one district. The fact that the satisfaction rating was about ten percentage points higher among Corps project managers than among contractor project managers jumped out at me and, after the presentation, I had a conversation with the Corps project manager in which I asked him about this discrepancy and why Corps project managers might like partnering more than contractors. He said, "Well, partnering is great until you run out of budget." With that simple comment, he highlighted my point. Many of the "solutions" for team-related problems only gloss over the problem without changing underlying agendas. Because of this, they might contribute to some success but are not a true solution to the problem of purpose in projects.

Project Companies are another form of project organization. Unlike partnering, project companies have been around for a long time. These usually have been created for massive projects that are in the interest of many stakeholders but beyond the resources of any specific stakeholder.

Trans-oceanic telecom cables are one example. Various telephone companies and contractors and other involved parties actually create a company for the purpose of building the project.

These companies have taken many forms over the years and going into a series of examples is beyond my intent here. However, the idea of a joint venture (JV) style company is one that might form the basis for a way to suitably align project purpose among stakeholders should the project warrant it based on factors such as complexity, size, scope, cost, and benefit. Such a company would likely include the owner or owners, the construction manager and first tier subcontractors, the architect/engineer and first tier sub-consultants. The structure would need to carefully balance the need for the owners to have significant say in the project with a need to not allow the owners to just automatically veto everything. The owners would need to be willing to become true joint participants even though they are both JV partners and end-state project owners. Although, in some situations, the entire project company might end up owning, operating, and maintaining the facility and the project "owners" end up being customers.

The **Skunkworks** approach is another example of how companies have attempted to resolve project issues by ensuring that team members are committed to the same goals. First pioneered by Lockheed Martin for aircraft development, a Skunkworks approach attempts to fully integrate an interdisciplinary team by isolating them from the typical constraints of the parent organization. Apple also implemented this approach during the development of the Macintosh computer. While this approach has mostly been applied to new product development projects, it was also implemented for a construction project with reportedly good results in terms of quality, cost, and schedule[15]. For this project, the key elements of the skunkworks approach were:

- Clear mission focus.
- Extensive up-front planning.
- Careful analysis of customer needs.
- Early involvement of key stakeholders such as equipment vendors.
- Team empowerment.
- Rule breaking (not doing things just because they have been done that way before).

It should not be surprising that these elements resemble a systems approach. By isolating a team and all of its members and focusing them on the project, the originators of this concept hit upon some of the elements of a systems approach. The key is to understand why these elements work to enable their application across a wider range of projects. And systems thinking explains why these elements worked, as well as why projects fail.

Integrated Project Delivery is another approach that exhibits elements of purpose alignment. The American Institute of Architecture (AIA) guidance document describes this approach as:

*a project delivery approach that integrates
people, systems, business structures and
practices into a process that collaboratively
harnesses the talents and insights of all
participants to optimize project results,
increase value to the owner, reduce waste,
and maximize efficiency through all phases
of design, fabrication, and construction.*[16]

The principles of this approach include:

- Mutual respect and trust.
- Mutual benefit and reward.
- Collaborative innovation and decision making.
- Early involvement of key participants.
- Early goal definition.
- Intensified planning.
- Open communication.
- Appropriate technology.
- Organization and leadership.

Compared to some of the other approaches mentioned above, this approach is fairly new. I have been involved in analysis of two projects that used this approach and neither were highly successful. While this is anecdotal data rather than statistical, I noticed some of the same issues with these projects as with other more traditional projects. I attributed this to two significant factors:

1. The inability of the organizations involved to truly break out of their traditional project mindset so that problems set off competing agendas.
2. The inadequacy of the contract documents to enforce true alignment of purpose.

An understanding of systems thinking, of the "why" behind the "principles", as well as the principles and tools in this book would enhance this approach in the future and contribute to greater success as an innovative format for future projects.

Team Incentives and Bonuses

One area that has not been adequately explored is the area of team incentives and bonuses. Typically, in a construction contract, the language forbids the contractor or construction manager from charging its personnel bonuses against the project. From a legal perspective, this makes sense in that project bonuses should come out of a company's profits and not just be a cost passed on to the owner. Such an approach can have the effect of incentivizing project personnel to make the project successful – for the organization paying the bonus. This works so long as the contractor's purpose is truly aligned with the owner's. When it is not, the contractor's project manager could get a bonus for defeating the purpose of the overall project.

One way to change this dynamic would be to contractually limit the contractor's ability to give bonuses to key project personnel involved with the project and to allow the owner to directly incentivize these individuals based on overall project performance. In order to work, the contractor must be committed to the project's purpose – but this is essential for project success anyway. Let the lawyers work out the legalese but this is one example where doing things differently than before can positively impact project success by aligning purpose above all.

The "non-controllable" elements of the system

In the model that we looked at in Chapter 13, Regulatory Agencies and Local Communities are shown as being outside the project boundary while in the operating environment for the system. Where these elements are cooperative and supportive of the project, they are almost, but not quite, parts of the project from a social systems standpoint. But at what point do these elements switch from being almost parts of the system to being challenges to the system's success?

While it is difficult to succeed with a project when the local agencies are against it, some project teams have done it. Rather than a battle, consider ways to at least partially get these elements of the operating environment on board with your project. While you might be able to fight city hall and win, it is better if you do not have to fight at all.

Putting your project on purpose

Project management research repeatedly identifies similar sets of success factors and most revolve around teams and their people rather than better budgeting or scheduling. But it is not enough to say that a project must have a "climate of trust" or "teamwork". That is like saying that a person must breathe oxygen to live. It is self-evident but does not say much about the "how" of effective project management. One study stated it in a way that is almost begging for a systems approach by defining alignment as:

> *"The condition where appropriate project participants are working within acceptable tolerances to develop and meet a uniformly defined and understood set of project*

*objectives. These project objectives must
meet business requirements and the overall
corporate strategy."[17]*

There is a reason why this is one of the longest chapters in the book. In the movie, *City Slickers*, Mitch, played by Billy Crystal, asked Curly, the old cowboy played by Jack Palance, about the secret of life. Curly replied that it was just "one thing". Mitch asked the obvious question, "What's the one thing?". And Curly replied that that is what YOU have to figure out. Arguably, the "one thing" is your purpose in life and that is what you have to figure out. With projects, your purpose is at least partially defined before you start the project. The secret of projects, the "one thing", is to ruthlessly align every aspect of your project toward accomplishing that purpose – your team, your resources, your planning, every single part. Putting your project on purpose is the foundation for success and the root of all that is to come. But, just like life, it is not enough by itself. Consider the next design principle – Coordinated Effort.

18. Coordinated Effort

How much redundancy is built into most projects? I am not certain but I suspect that there is a lot when it comes to the "soft costs" of project management, supervision, estimating, project controls, safety, etc. Let us look at a hypothetical example.

Imagine a data center project in which one element is an emergency power system (backup generators, switching gear, etc.). At some point in the project, the designer probably did an estimate of how much this element of the project would cost. In addition, the contractor did an estimate of the cost of this element as part of their guaranteed maximum price (GMP) agreement. Finally, the contractor puts the electrical work out to bid and each of the bidders also does an estimate for the emergency power system. Let us assume that each estimate was perfectly accurate (really?) and that no changes were made in the design specifications from the designer's initial estimate to bid time (in your dreams!), three different parties incurred the cost of the same estimate. This is redundancy. On top of this redundancy, the party most qualified to do the estimate (the electrical contractor) knows the least about the system in terms of its ultimate needs and uses at the time it does its estimate. And, this does not even consider that if the electrical contractor fully understood the needs behind the design, it might be able to propose a better and more cost-efficient way to fulfill those needs.

And this is just one example. Estimating, scheduling, quality management, oversight, project management, etc. are all done redundantly through the many layers of a traditional project. Then we bring in other parties, like an owner's representative. They are generally there because the owner lacks construction expertise or capacity and cannot really trust the agenda of the contractor.

Coordination is the process of organizing people and organizations so that they work together effectively and efficiently. For our purposes, a project should be organized so that all important aspects of execution and risk are covered while ensuring minimal overlapping efforts to minimize cost duplication.

Coordinated effort exhibits the following characteristics:

- Early involvement of all major stakeholders.
- Well-designed procedures with clearly designated roles and responsibilities, with responsibilities assigned based on the best ability to perform those responsibilities.
- Balanced and appropriate experience/ expertise between the parties involved.
- Risks allocated based on the best ability to manage specific categories of risk (more to come in Chapter 25 on re-thinking project Controls).
- Minimized redundancy and duplication of effort (which can only be accomplished if everybody is working toward the same purpose).

How much does Lack of Coordinated Effort cost?

The "soft" side of a project, management, design, and supervision, includes design, estimating, scheduling, project management, supervision, QA/QC, and administration at all levels of the project including the major stakeholders as well as subcontractors and vendors.

If the total cost of a sample project is $100 million then likely soft costs include:

- 0.5 – 1% for owner's internal management
- 0.5 – 1% for owner's representative
- 7% for A/E – little in the way of "materials" so let us say 6% is soft.
- 5-10% for CM's field overhead (including both materials and equipment – trailers and paper – as well as personnel and general conditions and general requirements.)
- 1-3% for CM's fee (including profit and home office overhead)

These add up to 13-21% of the $100 million is being spent on these soft costs or, for discussion's sake, an even $15 million. Of the remaining $85 million, I will assume an even split between purchased materials and equipment and trade labor.

Each materials and equipment vendor has their own internal management costs directly related to this project. Even if the variable costs of vendor management only equal 2% then that is 0.85 million of the 42.5 million. In addition, each trade contractor typically has its own management and supervision and field overhead If this is only 5% then it equals $2.125 million.

Just considering what we have estimated so far for this $100 million project, soft costs are just under $18 million or 18% of the whole. And I believe that this number is conservative on most projects. How much of this number is redundant and could be eliminated on a project where the major parties were working toward the same purpose and the entity best able to do a particular piece of work had the responsibility for that work. In addition, the possible opportunities are incalculable as each part of the system lends its own unique expertise toward the goal of optimizing the whole project.

Project owners sometimes try to push off all project risk onto other parties. The entire project then revolves around those other parties pushing back and trying to divest themselves of their responsibilities. On the other hand, projects in which no one has risk except for the owner tend toward significant budget overruns and delays. The time to design procedures is early in the project, once all the key team members are in place (and in alignment). Well-crafted procedures help to clarify responsibilities and reinforce the overall sharing of project risk and coordination of the work effort.

A project in which the owners or other key stakeholders are ignorant of the overall necessities and risks of project management might seem like a bonanza to the contractor but seldom ends well for anyone. While it might seem obvious that "coordinated effort" is essential to project success, the courts are full of projects where this principle was not followed. And those costs can far exceed what we have discussed as soft project costs due to redundancy. They can include costs due to labor productivity losses, schedule delays, excessive change orders, and even contractor defaults.

19. Effective Communication

Open, honest, and effective communication seems like another truism for project management. And yet, how often is communication meant to be open, honest, and effective rather than provoking, hiding, manipulative, risk-transferring, or an exercise in covering one's backside? Fortunately for your project, you have eliminated concern for hiding, manipulation, risk transfer and CYA exercises by aligning purpose and coordinating effort. Effective communication is the next principle to be built into your project social system.

Effective communication ensures that team members have the information they need to make the best decisions relative to their roles and responsibilities and that those decisions are disseminated in a timely manner and with any assumptions identified and presented transparently to the rest of the team. Communication should build on the following principles:

- Trust among team members.
- Well-designed formal lines of communication.
- Open, informal lines of communication.
- Transparent assumptions and intentions.
- Recording of decisions (essential to learning. and adaptation discussed later in Chapter 22).

Each aspect of an effectively built and honestly executed communications plan builds on every other aspect. Distrust only breeds further distrust. But open, honest, and effective communication builds on itself as well and can lead to early problem detection and resolution and more successful implementation of the project.

Automating a process to make it more efficient only helps if the process is already effective. However, the continued development and improvement of project documentation software and web-based solutions provides a ready tool for ensuring that all parts of your project system have access to the communications that they need.

20. Detailed Planning

"The really nice thing about not planning is that failure comes as a complete surprise and is not preceded by long periods of worry and depression!"--- Anonymous

Project management research as well as my own experience indicates that the best opportunity to influence the cost of a project (downward at least) is in the early phases of the project. Once project execution begins, the minimum level of cost for the project is already determined. Although poor execution can always increase the costs beyond what you would like. The Detailed Planning part of the project is the "thinking" part and includes what I refer to as meta-planning as well as technical design and execution planning.

Meta-planning occurs before the traditional project planning phase and it includes:

- Project conception/selection.
- Selection of the project purpose and alignment of that purpose with the parent organization's goals.
- Design of the project as a system to accomplish the purpose including the determination of the project organization and the selection of the project team.
- And the development of the meta-plan describing how the activities necessary to accomplish the purpose will be planned.

The meta-planning phase should be conceptually segregated from the operational and technical planning that comes later so that conscious attention is paid to the social system itself before means are discussed.

Detailed planning includes:
- Organizational design (team membership, roles and responsibilities, project controls, etc.).
- Contracting strategy.

- Risk management.
- Procurement planning.
- Integrated project execution documents.
- Early technical design and engineering.
- And the clarification of critical assumptions.

Planning costs little compared to execution. A qualified team could spend a year on planning a project without significantly impacting the overall budget. Too many project stakeholders want to rush to get shovels in the ground before they know where they are going. This contributes to costly change orders, work interferences, and misalignments between budgets, expectations, and reality.

Ackoff's approach to planning is called backwards planning and it is similar to the approach used in the military in that you begin with the desired end in mind and work backwards to where you are today to determine the best way to accomplish that end.

This approach is also embedded in idealized design, which is a useful tool at various points in the project, and is described at length in Chapter 24. Idealized design can be applied in the meta-planning phase, as well as for technical design and execution planning.

Detailed Planning for all three aspects of your project (meta-planning, technical design, and execution) will position the project for effective and efficient execution, the subject of the next chapter.

21. Effective and Efficient Execution

Building upon the detailed planning described in the previous chapter, the project team should be designed to enable effective and efficient execution. Originally, I thought of this as rapid execution. And while some projects can be completed more rapidly than others, clearly one of the goals should be to perform the execution phase as rapidly as possible while remaining effective or on purpose.

Most of us have probably seen the TV show, Extreme Home Makeover, in which a crew takes a family from their home and sends them on a week-long vacation. Meanwhile, the crew demolishes the home and builds a new one, along with donated assistance from contractors and volunteers. The well-known charity, Habitat for Humanity, celebrates teams that can build a spec house in the least time with the world record being around 4 hours from start to finish.

Finally, housing contractors can compete to build a house the fastest. They typically plan for months and build in hours. Each of these provides an example of rapid execution in residential construction. Each also relies heavily on the sort of detailed planning described in the previous chapter. Rapid execution of the project typically costs less and benefits the project owner more than extended or even "paced" progress.

Rapid execution does not necessarily imply an earlier start date. This is not a call to get "shovels in the ground" as quickly as possible. Instead, rapid execution is an attempt to minimize the duration of the execution period of the project. A factory that can be built in twelve months will cost more if built in eighteen. Time is almost always money. Extended execution times can incur greater management, inefficiency, and carrying costs as well as the lost opportunity from not having a completed facility. The keys to rapid execution often include the following:

- Upfront focus on detailed planning covered in the previous chapter.
- Well done engineering and a well-understood scope of work.
- Early involvement of stakeholders who are critical to execution.

- Modularization and off-site fabrication where possible, or the ability to take advantage of other construction innovations as they become available.

- Minimization of cushions built into the project schedule and proactive float management at the project level.

- Procurement of long-lead items and careful integration of procurement, materials management, and equipment staging.

- Bringing in the right parts of the team (including trade contractors) at the right times to minimize inefficiencies and overlap.

- Minimization of changes and timely management of changes when they occur.

- Constant work to validate assumptions and adjust plan if they prove to be invalid (as described in Chapter 22 on learning and adaptation).

- Efforts to make assumptions self-fulfilling by making them happen. For example, if a critical cost assumption is based on the current price of steel and that price is volatile - buy it now to lock in the price.

What is effective, efficient, and even "rapid" for your projects will differ. However, take the time to focus on building effective and efficient execution into your project. And when your plan hits a road-block, learn and adapt.

22. Learning and Adaptation

No plan, however detailed, can be perfect. In warfare, there is a relevant quote that says that "No plan survives first contact with the enemy." This is true of any planning. No one can perfectly predict what will happen during the course of the project. And while our approach focuses on assumptions rather than forecasts, not every assumption will prove to be true. Likewise, not every decision made during the project will prove to be sound.

To address this situation, the project team should be designed to be a learning organization. This does not mean that the detailed planning described in Chapter 20 is not essential. Instead, it means that as the project team performs detailed planning, it should incorporate an ability to learn and adapt into the core of the project. In this approach, properly designed project controls become early warning signals that key project assumptions require modification. The team records decisions (along with the assumptions, reasons for the decision, and expected outcomes) so that decisions might be modified later if conditions are found to be different than expected. And, lessons learned from similar projects are incorporated wherever relevant.

Uncertainty leads to Assumptions

Assumptions are the bridge over uncertainty that lead to action. Uncertainty in planning requires assumptions. You cannot act without assumptions but assumptions might be wrong. It is inherently impossible to predict the future. If you can predict the future then get out of this business now – run from construction as fast as you can because you can find much easier means of making money. But the fact is that you cannot predict the future.

If you knew that any specific problem was going to occur on your project – it would not be a problem.

Essentials of Learning and Adaptation

What does learning and adaptation mean? learning and adaptation can only occur when you have made an error either with regard to your overall goals (in this case the purpose of your project), your underlying assumptions, or your expected results.

Learning occurs when you discover that the actual results do not match your expectations or your assumptions. As a result, what you are doing to get to your goal is not working either at all or as well as you expected. Adaptation is what happens when you make a decision to modify your course of action based upon that learning and implement the decision and monitor its results. Of course, this could potentially lead to more learning should your decision prove to be in error. A decision to do nothing, or to not take a certain course of action, can be a learning experience. As discussed in Chapter 14, errors can be of omission as well as commission. In fact, errors of omission are usually worse than errors of commission.

The only way that a social system can learn and adapt is if its errors are made and then detected – the sooner the better. If the organization is working openly toward its purpose, then every decision-maker needs to understand this concept. Behavior designed to hide errors will only be more likely to lead to project failure. As described in Chapter 5 on competing agendas, when an engineering firm tried to cover up several of its design errors it led to overall project delays, increased costs, and eventual litigation thus costing far more to the owner than a quick recognition of the errors and a good decision to fix them.

Implementing Learning and Adaptation

According to Russell Ackoff, a learning and adaptation system must exhibit five characteristics:

1. Identification and formulation of threats, opportunities, and problems.
2. Decision making – determining what to do about threats, opportunities, and problems.
3. Implementation.
4. Control – monitoring performance and modifying actions
5. Acquisition or generation, and distribution of the information necessary to perform the other four functions[19]

Risk Management for Learning and Adaptation

The above process for learning and adaptation actually resembles the project risk management process which requires risk identification, analysis, management (including the decisions about what to do about the risk and implementation of those decisions), and monitoring of the risk. The formal definition of risk already includes both opportunities and threats. If we modify the focus slightly to include project assumptions, then risk management tools can provide a ready mechanism for project learning and adaptation.

Part of this process will be to identify critical assumptions. An assumption is critical if it will have a material impact on the project should it prove to be invalid. Looking for critical assumptions in the project might provide some unexpected results.

Let us look at a possible example of one such assumption. In a building schedule, let us assume that the critical path does not go through concrete masonry but that concrete masonry is only ten days behind the critical path. Clearly, the durations of concrete masonry activities in the schedule are dependent upon the productivity of the masons. That productivity is based on an assumption. So how critical is that assumption? A sensitivity analysis might show that if the masons only achieve 90% of their planned productivity, their activities will use their slack and will become the project's critical path, delaying the project by three weeks. Is this assumption about masonry labor productivity critical? It would seem to be so assuming that a 3-week delay to the project is considered significant enough to be material to overall success. How likely is it that somebody actually asks the question in a project team that is not focused on assumptions and risks?

Unfortunately, risk management tools are often unequally applied or not applied at all across projects even though they provide a potential path forward to the implementation of a L&A system. Chapter 25, on re-thinking project controls, will discuss the application of risk management as part of a systems approach to projects.

Part 5
Tools for
Success

A common mistake that people make when trying to design something completely foolproof is to underestimate the ingenuity of complete fools.
--- Douglas Adams

Part 5 – Tools for Success

23. Participative Team Selection

Team selection is a critical component of project success. From a social systems perspective, picking the team is the equivalent of picking the parts of the system. But even without resorting to systems thinking, studies of capital projects have repeatedly shown that the individuals and organizations that make up the team are critical to the success of the project.

Unfortunately, parent organizations often put less thought into the team selection process than they put into the color of the building's façade. Why is selection so critical? Expertise is important but not the only (or even most important reason). More important than expertise is the ability of the team to work together fluidly. In a system, the interactions can be more important than the parts.

Team selection and member interaction are doubly important because every part has strengths and weaknesses. An effective system ensures that the weaknesses of one part or team member are compensated for by the strengths of others. Think about marriage – love at first sight is not likely to work well.

The goals of the selection process are:

1. To develop a strong team that covers all key areas of the project.
2. To involve key players early in the planning process.
3. To put together a team capable of working well together.
4. To achieve buy-in and commitment from both organizational and individual team members.

The participative team selection process described below is designed to reach these goals. This process is divided into two phases. Phase 1 involves the pre-qualification of three designers (architect and/or engineer depending on the type of facility) and three builders (construction contractors). It is an initial cut based on qualifications. Phase 2 involves the selection of the designer and the builder based upon participation of all seven parties (3 designers, 3 builders, and the parent organization). The process as described is focused on construction projects but, with a little imagination, could be adapted to other project types.

Phase 1 of the Selection Process

Phase 1 is the initial cut based on qualifications. The goal is to make sure that all of the participants in Phase 2 have the necessary technical qualifications so that the focus there can be how well they will work together. Phase 1 begins with a needs analysis to identify the primary qualifications needed and will probably end either a Request for Qualifications (RFQ) document or an informal equivalent. Critical pieces of information at this point include:

- A clear description of the project's purpose. This should not be a surprise if you have read this far.
- Program elements as known: purpose, location (if selected), approximate size, etc. This is a description of the physical attributes of the facility needed keeping in mind that the team has yet to perform any design work.
- Target cost or budget: Chapter 26 will discuss target costing in more depth. But this number is derived directly from the business case used to justify the project prior to deciding to

advance the process. It is the assumed cost used to make the decision. It, along with the benefit part of the cost/ benefit analysis, answers the question of whether or not you should do the project.

- Target deadline: Similar to the target cost but in time rather than money.
- A description of the selection process to be employed.
- Identification of the selection criteria to be used.
- A description of expertise/ experience including experience with your type of facility and work in your region/ area of the country.
- References from owners/clients but also from non-client parties (e.g. subcontractors, vendors) that worked with that organization in order to get 360 degree feedback.
- Contractor: Health & safety ratings.
- And a copy of this book (just kidding – sort of).

Once you have the information from potential designers and builders, your team of key stakeholders should review the information. The goal is to whittle down the master list to 3 designers and 3 builders that are well qualified to do this type of project in your area.

At a minimum, the team should evaluate the candidates based on conventional criteria such as:

- Experience with similar projects in your region.
- Experience in your industry.
- Success with those projects (definitely check references of owners with similar projects before adding a firm to your shortlist) to include questions about ability to meet budget and deadlines, ease or difficulty of working relationships, and disputes and litigations.
- Safety ratings of builders.

Remember, you ultimately intend to create a successful team incorporating these organizations, so it is important to consider not just the organization but the project managers and key personnel who were involved in any reference projects. In addition, any clues about how they have worked as a team in the past should be carefully considered. Examples might include litigations or disputes.

Before moving on to a description of Phase 2 however, I would like to put in a brief word on design-build and Engineer-Procure-Construct (EPC) entities and why I tend to avoid them in these processes. I have been privy to the inner workings of both types of entities and have not been impressed with the quality of their internal interactions. And the problem for the owner is that these interactions will be hidden or opaque. Although proponents of these processes argue that they eliminate some of the problems that you want to eliminate in your organizational design, in fact, many times the problems just go underground. The fact that it is out of sight should not give you peace of mind. If you can work with such an organization to make their processes and interactions more transparent, then you might be able to make it work. Making these processes transparent will be more difficult than in a situation where the organizations are separate and contractually bound to interact in the ways that you need them to interact – and to do so transparently.

Once you have narrowed your list down to three designers and three builders, it is time to begin Phase 2 of the selection process.

Phase 2 of the Selection Process

Phase 2 involves the selection of the final designer and builder for your team. The overall goal of this process is to involve all the participants in such a way that the final candidates are likely to be able to assist in the design of an effective project team. In this phase, the selections will be done concurrently unlike a more traditional selection process in which the designer is selected long before the contractor is selected.

A range of variations for the process described here might work. But one critical component is that each of the candidate organizations must provide their actual team members that will be assigned to the project. They cannot be allowed to do a "bait and switch" in which they put forth one team to win the contract and then change it once the project is underway. Of course, personnel might change during the project but the owner should seek to keep the team together as designed and should try, where possible, to implement a smaller scale version of this process to help select and onboard replacement team members.

During Phase 2, each candidate builder team spends time at each candidate designer's office and vice versa. This could be a few hours to a day and should be designed to allow each team to get to know the other, see their offices, and possibly brainstorm how the project might be better accomplished in terms of staffing, communications, controls, reporting, value engineering, constructability studies, etc. A representative from the owner's organization will be present to observe these sessions and their interactions as well as to record their findings. One topic that could form the basis of these discussions could be one or more previous projects that the designer and the builder worked on together before along with successes, failures, and lessons learned.

Each designer will rate each builder and vice versa. The representative from the owner will also meet with and rate each team. So, each candidate organization will end up with four ratings. Remember, all the organizations have been evaluated already for their ability to do the technical aspects of the project. In this phase, each organization will be evaluated according to four criteria:

- Innovativeness.
- Ability to interact.
- Willingness to interact with the group being rated.
- Overall success of the interactions.

A number of rating systems could be used including a 1-5 or 1-10 scale rating with comments as well as a ranking where each of the three designers rating three candidate builders ranks them in order (and vice versa). Ultimately, the owner is trying to determine which combination would be able to work together best on their project team. While most processes on this project will be designed to be transparent, for this process, the owner might decide that the ratings received from each of the designers and builders for the others will be kept confidential and, if so, should make this clear to participants.

Once this process is complete and the final selection is made, design will begin – of both the project organization and, then, of the building or facility to be built. For both of these, another systems tool, idealized design, can be a good way to start.

24. Idealized Design

Russell Ackoff's Idealized Design process is well suited to the systemic design of a project organization as well as the design of the performance specifications (and even some of the more detailed design features) of the physical facility to be constructed. Idealized design helps to align purpose as well as to develop buy-in among the key stakeholders. With regard to the physical facility, it helps to ensure that the final design incorporates the critical needs of the team and that it aligns well with the overall purpose (or business case) of the project.

Idealized design is an interactive planning process that consists of "the design of a desirable present and the selection or invention of ways of approximating it as closely as possible"[20]. Key characteristics of this process are that it is:

- **Participative/Interactive:** The process inherently develops alignment or "buy-in" because it is open and interactive involving all of the key stakeholders in the design of the system of which they will be parts.

- **Creative:** By starting from scratch and identifying what is ideally desired, this process frees people from some of their self-imposed constraints, enabling them to generate more creative, efficient, and effective ideas.

- **Ideal-seeking:** The process fosters an ideal-seeking system that is able to learn and adapt to changing conditions in accordance with its purpose. While different organizations will necessarily design different project social systems based upon their purposes, needs, and resources, well designed projects will tend to seek similar ideals such as: the design principles in this book.

The Idealized Design Process

As developed by Ackoff, this methodology has two parts: *idealization* and *realization*. During the idealized planning part, the participants envision an ideal system (in this case a social system for achieving project ends). During realization, they then try to design the means to bring about this reality by working backwards from the ideal. They first ask, "Where would you be right now if you could redesign everything?" That question is followed by, "How do you get to that state?"

The Idealized Design process follows two idealization steps which are taken to understand where you are and where you would rather (or ideally) be, and four realization steps which are to get you there:

Idealization

1. **Formulating the mess:** In this step, your team evaluates where you are and identifies where and why things will eventually fail if they wee to continue on the current path. This understanding creates an urgency for change. If you are designing your project organization you will be looking at how you have "always done it before" and the problems that you have encountered or foresee with continuing to do it that way. Some of this has been done for you in this book. If you are designing your facility then you will look at problems with existing facilities and what is broken that is leading you to undertake this project. This is the mess that you are in. It includes all the aspects of your current situation that make you less effective and/or efficient.

2. **Ends planning:** In this step, your team determines where you would ideally like to be right now if you could design your organization to accomplish its purpose (the ideal state). This redesign assumes a blank slate and should only be limited by constraints of legality and technical feasibility. This step will result in a set of specifications (for your organization or your facility) and will include prioritization of those specifications based on their importance. It will also identify and address the gap between your ideal state and your current mess.

Realization

3. **Means planning:** Means planning begins to answer the question, how will we get to our desired state? What steps are necessary to get us from here to there?

4. **Resource planning** answers the question of what do we need to get to the desired step? Based on our prioritization and our available resources, what should be our focus? How will we begin to approximate our idealized design with the resources we have? Note that it is often the case when designing a physical facility using idealized design that the full idealized design cannot be realized with

available resources. That is why prioritization is essential and this overall process is iterative in nature.

5. **Design of implementation:** In this step, the team plans the execution of the new design.

6. **Design of controls:** Here, the team designs the controls that will enable the new system to learn and adapt and that will ensure that implementation is on track.

Mechanics of the Process

Typically, a series of facilitated sessions are conducted to work through the idealized design process. These sessions include key representative stakeholders to ensure that the final design (either of organization or facility) meets the needs of the team and the purpose of the project. Both the design of the team and the design of the facility should involve key stakeholders from outside the parent organization including the designer and the builder.

Idealized Design Applications

This process can be applied to the design of your organization as well as the physical design of the facility that you plan to build. A friend of mine, Jason Magidson, co-authored a book called *Idealized Design* which describes how to apply this process to a range of situations. Dozens of organizations have employed idealized design to successfully redesign themselves in addition to its applications to physical facilities.

One case of physical facility design is instructive. Jason's team worked with a major global retailer to apply this design to one of their new flagship stores. During the process, the team identified specifications such as:

- Ease of finding what you are looking for.
- Ease of navigation eliminating disorientation.
- Convenience by including related items together.
- Fast checkout and self-checkout capabilities.
- A relaxing and pleasant experience.

The team came up with a truly innovative store design based upon these and other criteria that they developed. These criteria and specifications were then further developed by the architect and then built. When the store was completed, sales were twice initial expectations. Unfortunately, due to management changes, later stores did not incorporate this innovative design and, were you to shop there, you would probably recognize (as I have) that the current design is a failure that achieves the opposite of the above design specifications.

The Idealized Design process assists with not only achieving a better design that takes into account the parent organization's (and maybe customers') needs, it also achieves buy-in by involving key stakeholders in the design process. Chapter 27 touches upon another tool critical to involving stakeholders and achieving buy-in as far as the physical facility is concerned, design visualization. In addition, Chapter 26 discusses the application of a targeting approach to your project including all aspects of your project controls (estimate, budget, schedule, etc.). It is similar in some aspects to the idealized design process described here and dovetails nicely with it.

Part of the idealized design of your project organization will undoubtedly involve specifications for project controls. In the next chapter, I discuss how we can re-think project controls based on our new understanding of the needs and requirements of a social system.

25. Re-thinking Project Controls

"It's tough to make predictions, especially about the future." --- Yogi Berra

Given my earlier discussions and criticisms of project controls (scheduling, budgeting, estimating, etc.), you may have thought that we would never get to this point. But project controls, *properly established and used*, provide a necessary and invaluable tool for systemic project management. Project controls can provide the project organization with the learning and adaptation mechanisms it needs to successfully accomplish the project. Once an effective system is designed (the project organization), well-designed project controls can make it both more effective and efficient. How are project controls used in projects?

Unfortunately, project controls are often implemented with a view toward limiting liability (CYA!), shifting risk or responsibility (CYA!), or merely meeting contract requirements (CYA!). Sometimes the resulting data and analyses are actually thinly veiled delusions of both self and others. I once worked on a case involving a significant schedule delay. In the course of the investigation, several important things came to light:

- The project schedule's critical path did not reflect the reality of the project. In fact, the types of activities one would expect to see as critical for this facility were not. The critical path had in fact been rigged to run through a series of activities that should have been less important so that it was dependent on an owner milestone. By doing this, the contractor thought they would gain more time as they thought the owner would likely miss the milestone.

- The schedule reflected an unchanged end date until a few months before the end date, and then it showed about six months of delay. Analysis revealed that the schedule had been modified each month to make it show the "right" end date regardless of what was actually happening. When questioned about this, the head scheduler for the contractor replied, "My management does not like to see negative float" (i.e. schedule reports that show delayed activities).

- When the project superintendent was asked for his opinion of the schedule, he replied that "It is for management. It's no good for me."
- The owner received monthly schedule updates from the contractor but they were paper reports missing critical information for a proper schedule evaluation. They received the native electronic file as well, but did not have the software to open it.

For this project, the project schedule, a critical project control, was rigged to shift risk and responsibility (CYA!), was manipulated to hide delay (CYA!), and, thus, was not useful to the people who should have needed it to run the project! It was a tool for delusion for both the contractor and the owner. While most flawed uses of project controls are probably not this bad, many of them do the same thing to lesser degrees. When you use project controls primarily to shift risk and responsibility and to protect yourself from liability then you are replacing Oz's yellow brick road with a red critical path that leads to the same place – a fraud barely hidden behind a curtain. Do not be left shrieking, "Pay no attention to the project reality behind the curtain!"

This chapter should provide you with a new way of thinking about project controls as part of systemic project management by first describing decision making and its relationship to project controls, the characteristics of systemic project controls, the use of risk management as a framework, open processes, and target budgeting and scheduling. Many of the nuts and bolts of project controls will remain the same while the overall guiding approach and focus changes. The nuts and bolts are beyond the scope of this chapter (and this book) but understanding the new approach and focus is critical to successful systemic project management.

Decision Making and Systemic Project Controls

Decisions made early in your project both have more impact and also constrain decisions made later. This truth is readily apparent in manufacturing. The decision to manufacture a high-end sports car rather than a low-end economy car already determines more about the project's costs than later, more detailed decisions such as how to finish the interior.

The same principle applies to construction projects. Pareto's 80/20 principle suggests that 80% of the minimum possible cost for your project is locked in by the time the project is 20% complete. But it might even be worse. Maybe a 90/10 rule. Or even 95/5. That means you must be on top of your project from Day 1. Your early decisions regarding the team that you are putting together for the project, the scope, the budget, the timing requirements, and technical design will impact your project more than your later ones.

Because personnel change and learning and adaptation is critical, a project controls system designed to capture decision records along with their critical assumptions and to test the validity of these assumptions as early as possible is essential.

In fact, the only way that learning and adaptation take place is when decisions are wrong, assumptions are flawed, or execution is poorly done AND these problems are identified and corrected. Behavior designed to pass the blame or protect a team member from liability can only lead to gaps in learning and adaptation and project problems that become more serious.

Characteristics of Systemic Project Controls

"Managers who don't know how to measure what they want settle for wanting what they can measure." – Russell Ackoff

In a systemic approach to project management, project controls provide the primary learning and adaptation mechanisms for the project organization. They do this by allowing for interactive and iterative planning that incorporates revised decisions based upon errors identified and fixed.

While the tools and techniques of these controls (cost management, scheduling, etc.) will look mostly like standard techniques, they will differ by being incorporated into an overall risk management framework that has been modified to record key decisions and to treat assumptions as risks.

When the tools are employed, the goal is not necessarily to get THE right answer, but to ask the RIGHT questions. For example, the project team might recognize the value of implementing an earned value management system to track costs and productivity. Earned value techniques include a variety of equations that can be solved to provide the team with an Estimate-At-Completion (EAC). Each of those equations has built-in assumptions. When used as part of a systemic approach, the goal would not be to determine which equation provides the true prediction. In fact, predictions are not the goal at all. From this perspective, the team should understand the assumptions that form the basis for each of the equations and use those assumptions to ask the right questions.

One EAC equation assumes that, regardless of what has happened to date, the rest of the project is on track to be completed with planned productivity. So, yes, some of our early assumptions were wrong or an unforeseen event occurred, but we are back on track and our earlier assumptions will hold true for the remainder of this project. When this equation is applied, the question becomes, is this a valid assumption? Is the problem fixed and over? Are there any indications that tell us that the assumptions about the remaining work are valid or not? And, of course, can we modify our plans to get us back on track? What assumptions would be required to determine that this was possible? And how soon can we know if they are correct? This is just one example of using project controls to ask the right questions rather than just to demonstrate that you have the right answer. This questioning approach enables learning rather than a false confidence based on cherry picking techniques to get the desired answer.

As we have already seen, a systemic approach to project controls will also include a preference for assumptions over predictions. The tools of prediction will still be employed but to validate and question assumptions. An important component of this approach includes the identification of all assumptions critical to the success of the project.

Risk Management as the Framework

A formal risk management process, with a few modifications, provides a ready framework for a project's need for learning and adaptation.

Risks, as typically defined, can be positive or negative. They can be opportunities or problems. Risk consists of two primary ingredients: probability and impact. Probability defines the likelihood that the specific risk will occur – without any intervention on your part. Impact tells us what will happen if the risk occurs. Will it cost money, delay the project, injure someone, or make the finished product fail?

An asteroid striking the center of your city impacts you (pun intended). As does a pie in the face. If you know that both were to happen tomorrow, which would catch more of your attention? That's the impact side of the equation.

Any risk you could dream of could impact your project, but some are more likely than others and some are worse than others. Fortunately, the most likely are not usually the worst imaginable.

A failed project could wallop your competitive advantage by sapping you of much needed time and capital while failing to meet the needs that drove you to undertake the project in the first place.

Effective traditional risk management is an iterative process that helps you answer these questions:

- What are our key risks?
- Are we focused on the risks that matter?
- Who is accountable for the key risks?
- What are we doing to manage those risks?
- Are resources aligned to our risk profile?
- Are we accepting an appropriate level of risk?
- Are we receiving a fair return on that risk?
- Who is monitoring the significant risks?
- How are we improving key controls so that we can recognize when our efforts are not working?
- Are we continuing to look for new risks in order to manage them or take advantage of them?

The traditional Risk Management Process has been described in a series of four to six steps by various sources but they all include the following elements:

1. **Planning** to determine who will run the risk management process, how reporting will be done, how it will tie into other areas of project

management or corporate processes (accounting, etc.), what resources will be devoted to the process, and the approach to be used.

2. **Risk Identification** to create a list of project risks. This list, typically referred to as a risk register, is often put together based on categories of risk (e.g. financial, regulatory, or environmental). The net should be widely cast during this step. Further steps can winnow the list to eliminate those that should not be on the register.

3. **Assessment and/or Analysis** to determine the two key facets of risk, probability and impact, with respect to the risks that you identified in the previous step. This step might involve qualitative approaches as well as quantitative techniques. Most likely, you will combine the two in a mix that is tailored to your needs and capabilities. The end goal of this step is a clear (albeit usually relative) understanding of how likely each risk is to occur and how much harm or benefit will accrue should it occur.

4. **Management or Response Planning** to decide what strategy you will implement for each of the risks you have identified and analyzed and who will have primary

responsibility for implementing the strategy. There are four primary strategies. You can try to give the risk to somebody else (*transfer* or *sharing*). This is commonly implemented contractually or by buying insurance. You can try to *avoid* the risk altogether through a variety of means depending on the type of risk. You might *mitigate* the risk or make it either less likely to happen or less impactful if it does happen. Or you might *accept* the risk. If you accept the risk, then you need to make sure you have additional funds allotted to handle the risk should it arise.

5. **Response Implementation** to execute the strategies that you decided to adopt for each risk during the last step. With those strategies should come actionable timeframes. This is when you act.

6. **Monitoring** to understand the status of your identified risks and to detect any previously unidentified risks that might be emerging. During this step, you use controls designed during your response planning as well as other project management tools and data sources to ensure that you are successfully managing your risks and identifying any new risks.

This process is already fairly well understood in terms of how to implement it on a project. It also ties in most of the other types of project controls around cost, schedule, and scope because they provide critical input as to risks. With the additional understanding that project assumptions are risks and that they need to be clearly identified, understood, and managed and that decisions need to be recorded, this process can be expanded to become the over-arching learning and adaptation process for the project.

Aspects of the project that might contain critical assumptions include:

- Codes, regulations and standards.
- Worker availability and skill levels.
- Materials/equipment availability and quality.
- Lack of existing infrastructure (hardware, software, facilities).
- Permits & regulatory requirements.
- Transportation & communications.
- Economic drivers (e.g. exchange rates).
- Software compatibility.
- Boundary conditions and other technical or engineering assumptions.
- Related work by others (e.g. utilities).
- Procurement schedules.
- Testing and operation.

But you should keep in mind that an assumption in any area can prove critical. I once worked on litigation in which the firm engineering and building the manufacturing facility acted upon a critical assumption about the chemical makeup and constituency of the soil upon which they were building. This resulted in differential heaving and settling of the facility once built and damages to the tune of tens of millions of dollars.

The importance of the idea that processes, decisions, and problems are understood throughout the project team cannot be understated.

Open Processes

Project controls processes employed in systemic project management should employ an "Open Books" approach. This approach is based on five principles.

1. Costs are real.
2. Transparency is paramount.
3. Business case determines design.
4. Design determines budget (or schedule).
5. Contingency for uncertainty.

Costs Are Real: This comment might seem ridiculous but it is amazing how many times owners or other project stakeholders seem to proceed with the attitude that they can get something for nothing. That does not work in reality. To quote Robert Heinlein, the paragon of science fiction, "There ain't no such thing as a free lunch." Every assumption has a cost. Every design feature has a cost. All project controls systems should be designed to reflect and report these costs as accurately as possible with the information at hand. It does no good to approve a conceptual design for a $200 million facility that cannot be built for $200 million. That creates disaster from the beginning rather than success.

Transparency Is Paramount: The processes are transparent to all the parties involved when assumptions, analysis techniques, constraints, estimates, and supporting documentation are open for review. The goal for any iteration is to come up with the best possible answer within caveats that are clearly understood and with assumptions and questions clearly defined. There should be no hidden costs in this process. There will be uncertain costs but those are handled by contingency described below.

Business Case Determines Design: The project's parent organization has a need that has turned into the purpose for the project. This need is supported by a business case. Some of the assumptions are around cost and/or schedule and some are around benefits. These assumptions ultimately determine some of the key design characteristics which (per the next principle) and those, per the next principle, determine the cost. This should be revisited on a regular basis. Original project approval was predicated on gaining certain benefits for certain costs. If those benefits cannot be achieved for the allotted cost then the project's approval should be reconsidered. A project that spends the allotted money while achieving less than the desired benefit is a failure.

Design Determines Budget (or Schedule): Design features added or subtracted lead potentially to costs (or schedule duration) added or subtracted. You cannot build a Mercedes for the cost of a Yugo. This principle relates to the first principle that costs are real however it builds on it by emphasizing that design decisions impact your ability to lower costs far more than construction or execution does. Once you have decided to build a wall of concrete blocks that is a certain height and length with specified reinforcement, there is a lowest possible cost that the builder cannot go below regardless of efficiency. It is always possible to increase costs through inefficiency but there is a lower limit to each building component that cannot be lowered. Some estimates are that 80% of the best possible cost are already decided when you are only 20% of the way through the project. I think it might even be 90%/ 10%. Without a doubt, the best way to impact your construction costs for the better is through better design from the beginning.

Contingency For Uncertainty: All designs and plans contain uncertainty. Regardless of how well you employ value engineering and constructability review processes, there will still be risk or uncertainty. This uncertainty should be accounted for with project contingency. A project with no contingency available is unlikely to be successful. Scheduling contingency is usually called *float* or *slack* but, for these purposes, works the same way.

Systemic project controls relate directly to the targeting approach described in the next chapter.

26. A Targeting Approach

Reverse planning involves starting with the operation's end state and working backward in time. Leaders begin by identifying the last step, the next-to-last step, and so on. They continue until they reach the step that begins the operation. It answers the question -- Where do we eventually want to be?
-- FM 3-21.10, US Army

Russell Ackoff's approach to systems thinking always emphasizes backwards planning. For example, in the idealized design process described in Chapter 24, you plan from the ideal back to how you can get there. As the above quote illustrates, this method should be familiar to those with a military background. *Target costing* is yet another backwards planning approach that has been used in manufacturing and can be modified to make your construction projects more successful.

The application of a targeting approach to your project and its estimate, budget, schedule, etc. means that you are beginning with the desired end (the ideal state) and working backwards from that end

This will start with the design of the facility. Idealized design provides a set of specifications and implementation plans. The business case provides constraints related to available resources and timeline. With a targeting approach, the design works backwards from those specifications and constraints to identify the necessary design components and how they can best be combined to accomplish the specifications while staying within the constraints. The involvement of the builder in this process provides insight into constructability and the potential impact of design decisions on the cost and the schedule. The goal is to design a facility that meets the specifications while not exceeding the constraints or, should that prove impossible, to provide that feedback to the owner as soon as possible.

It is imperative to remember two things during this process. First, as discussed under the section on open processes in the last chapter, costs are real. The team must not ignore real costs in order to pretend that the project's specifications are attainable within the set constraints. Those constraints are the result of the business case process. In some cases, they might be reconsidered should the benefit seem great enough. However, in others, if the project is not feasible within the constraints of the business case, it should NOT be built. At the very least, the approving parties should be given this information as early as possible to make this decision. Second, apparent cost cutting is not always real cost cutting and the involvement of the builder should help with this issue as well as help to bring innovative solutions to bear on achieving project goals.

One project with which I am familiar highlighted this principle. The procurement team was incentivized to cut the costs of procured items and ended up ordering several systems on a piecemeal component basis rather than as a completed and ready-to-plug-in system. They saved on apparent costs of procuring the items however the cost of assembling the components in the field proved to be much greater than the cost of shop fabrication. This resulted in a disastrous cost overrun and delay. Costs are real and not all cost cutting actually lowers costs. This example also illustrates one of the key points of systems thinking, that maximizing the performance of one part can decrease the performance of the whole.

In manufacturing, target costing is a process that allows a manufacturer to determine the price points, product development and manufacturing costs, and desired profit that it wants to achieve for its new product. So, for example, a camera company might develop a list of features that it would like to develop and implement for its new camera. It would make estimates (informed assumptions) regarding the costs to develop and manufacture such a camera. Market research would identify price points for which a camera with such features would be viable for the target market.

When applied to a construction process, target costing or scheduling begins with the desired specifications and the existing cost and schedule constraints. Then, typically, at set milestones, the team compares the design and its estimated costs to the project specifications and constraints to determine whether to proceed or whether drastic actions such as redesign are needed. In some industries, a stage-gate process is normally employed for projects. This can be readily adapted to incorporate the targeting approach described here.

A targeting approach will include:

- Value engineering to identify design alternatives that might lower costs.
- Constructability reviews to identify implementation issues or alternatives that

would cause cost increases or could provide ways to lower cost.

- Iterative design to reach the target cost as necessary.
- Regular approval points as described above.
- Estimates tied to specific design features with clearly defined assumptions (there are those assumptions again!).

While this discussion has focused more on costs, it also applies to the project schedule. In fact, schedules are often built from the beginning to the end rather than backwards from the desired end to the beginning. A targeting approach will change this and will allow for the schedule to be adjusted where possible to meet necessary business case constraints.

It is important to realize that this approach is only as good as the original business case. If it is based upon flawed assumptions (as to benefits and/or available resources) then the targeting approach should bring those to light as early as possible. And one possible solution would be the reconsideration of the business case by the approving parties.

One way in which people who are not design or construction professionals often end up with flawed assumptions is through their inability to adequately understand what the design features look like or accomplish. The next chapter, Design Visualization, describes this problem in more detail and discusses the importance of using available tools to mitigate it to the extent possible.

27. Design Visualization

"For now we see through a glass, darkly"
--- Saint Paul

Individuals required to make key design decisions vary greatly in their ability to visualize and understand the design and its ramifications, as though they are looking through a dark glass. This can result in massive disconnections between perceived needs and the final product and changes along the way that are costly in terms of both budget and time. Design visualization tools can provide the project team with the ability to remedy this problem.

A friend of mine is an architect who designed a school near me. There was a trend at the time to put metal roofs on schools and to use a very distinctive green color, kind of a kelly green. I am not sure how that began but my friend incorporated that color in the roof of the new school. One day, while the school was under construction, members of the building committee came to the site. The roof work was under way and probably one-third complete. They were horrified and called him immediately to complain about the color of the roof. He told me later that he did not say what came into his mind which was,

> *"The green was in the drawings you approved. It was in the specs that you approved. Which part of green didn't you understand?"*

My personal sense of aesthetics relating to the subtleties of color would not enable me to say with authority whether the green worked or not. But what is clear from this story is that, somehow, even with written specs, beautiful renderings (color drawings), and samples, this decision-making group missed a key element of the design.

A client of mine had a CEO that was known for walking into a project and ordering changes to work that was already under way or even completed. Such changes cost these owners as they implement mid-course corrections.

Changes during construction usually cost more than changes made during design. In fact, a useful rule of thumb is that a change order to a contractor during construction costs 15-20% more than the same change would have cost if it had been incorporated in the design initially. So, if you make $10 million worth of such changes in the course of the project then you have spent an extra $2 million. And this does not consider a change that actually requires demolition of completed work or any impacts to the project schedule. The simple but often underappreciated truth is that change during construction costs more than change during design.

Earlier, we discussed the use of the idealized design process to develop a design that propels the organization towards its purpose. But developing a shared vision may be impossible if we cannot see the same things. Individuals vary tremendously in their ability to 'see' and understand the design as portrayed by traditional design drawings.

In addition, people do not always know what they need, want, or what they would most benefit from unless they can experience it. Designs that affect work flow are especially problematic in this regard. A hospital client experienced an issue with the patient rooms on one of the floors. Hospitals have regular electrical outlets but also have outlets colored red. The ones that are red are tied into emergency backup power and are set aside for critical equipment that must be operable during a power outage. During construction, the rooms on one floor were well along when the head nurse toured the site. She walked into a room and noticed the placement of the red outlets and immediately realized that they could not go where they were being placed because the patient care model required critical equipment that would be located too far from the red outlets. As a result of this late realization, the red outlets in completed rooms were relocated and rewired. The nurse had approved the drawings showing their constructed locations. But being a layperson when it came to construction drawings, she was unable to properly visualize the impact of those locations when she approved them.

This lack of vision is not always one way. Designers do not always know how to turn an owner's vision into reality. Sometimes they say no when they should say yes. So, do not take no for an answer - at least not right away. The first no is usually too easy. It could really mean, "We haven't done it before." While there is no reason to reinvent the wheel, you should understand that a lot of design is the result of cutting and pasting elements from previous designs. Do not let your idealized design get lost during the translation process:

But even when the designer is true to the vision, the design can go awry. Too often, the design process incorporates an implicit assumption that users understand technical language. Drawings are one form of technical language. Written specifications are another. To the fluent, they say a lot. They might even enable the fluent to experience the design virtually and truly understand the impact of any decisions. To those who do not speak the language however, they might be incomprehensible. The project team must ensure that the design is as widely translated as possible. Careful consideration should be given to a variety of translating tools ranging from the technical to the traditional to the innovative.

The goal of using design visualization techniques is to allow design professionals to meet in the middle with other project stakeholders so that they can both agree on what will be built, and so that they can both understand the ramifications of their design decisions and the eventual impact on the completed project and the owner's project needs.

There are a range of tools in the design visualization toolbox and new ones are being invented as technology progresses. I have little doubt that, eventually, project stakeholders will be "touring" their project in virtual reality long before it is constructed.

- **Drawings and Specifications:** Traditional design and construction drawings typically provide overviews of the facility as well as breaking the design down into discipline (e.g. structural, electrical, mechanical, etc.) as well as a written description of the various design components and their requirements. These typically form the basis for the contract definition of what is being built but can be difficult for laypersons to understand.

- **Renderings** are traditional color drawings of either the entire or parts of the finished facility. More recently, computers have enabled designers to incorporate computer rendered drawings into a photo of the existing site and allow for "photoshopping" to show stakeholders what the facility will look like once complete.

- **Models** are the traditional 3D scale models that architects often created for buildings. If it has not already, I would expect 3D printing to bring down the cost of creating such models by eliminating a lot of the handwork and allowing the model to be completed more quickly and with greater levels of detail and accuracy.

- **Mockups** are full-size temporary constructions of specific design elements (e.g. a "typical" room layout). While expensive and needing of a location where they can be built (either on or off site), these allow stakeholders to see almost exactly what the design elements will be like when constructed.

- **3D Computer-Aided Design** allows for more detailed visualization of the design elements throughout the project. These tools include software that has been developed for specific needs such as checking for problems and conflicts in piping layouts in an industrial facility.

- **Building Information Modeling (BIM)** is a software-based process that incorporates computer designed drawings with a range of information about the construction and later even the operation of the building. With BIM, a team can evaluate progress as well as incorporate information critical to the long-term operation and maintenance of the facility.

There is a trade-off between the choice to use any particular method and the budget and available time (and sometimes the skillset of the designer). This cost should be weighed, however, against the ramifications of getting it wrong. And as computer and design technology progresses, the costs for the higher tech tools will continue to decrease.

BIM in particular is a leading-edge technology that has the ability to allow project teams to better perform design, coordinate the work in progress, and incorporate schedules and budgets into the visualization to better understand progress and productivity. While this is not the place to get into the nuts and bolts of BIM software, popular choices include Autodesk Revit and Navisworks, Synchro, and Trimble Vico depending on the purpose in mind.

If you can "see" it, you can probably agree to build it. If you cannot "see" it, you probably should call full stop.

The Beginning

"So let it be written, so let it be done."
--- Yul Brenner as Pharaoh
in The Ten Commandments

The Beginning

The goal of this book was not to provide you with ONE answer, or one way of doing things. But like Curly's "one thing" from *City Slickers*, PURPOSE is the glue that holds together a successful project and binds its team, processes, and tools together into a cohesive whole. While this true of all projects, there is not one exact way to design your specific team, processes, and tools. But designing them to support your purpose is essential.

I began this book by describing problems with the traditional view of project management and some of the common problems faced by projects then described systems thinking and its implications for social systems such as your project. Following that, I explained the seven design principles that follow from a systemic approach to project management and topped that off with a discussion of five different project tools and why they will help you succeed.

My goal was to provide you with a set of principles, an innovative way of looking at your projects, and some pointers that can assist you in developing your own successful project organization according to your own purpose. But you have to make them your own by following your "one thing." This is not the End, but the Beginning. You are not finishing a book but starting to look at your projects in a different way than you might have before.

Now. Seriously. Go DO it!

1. **Become** a systems thinker.
2. **Apply** the ideas you find here to create successful projects. **Modify** them as needed to fit your project needs.
3. **Involve** your team early and often to design your project in accordance with systems thinking principles (both the organization and the facility).
4. **Build** on your own experience **to innovate** ways that I have not thought of or included in this book.
5. And if you have any questions or need help – **contact me!** And we will work together to make sure that your projects are **on purpose.** That they follow your "one thing."

NOTES

1   The late Dr. Russell L. Ackoff was a pioneer and giant in the systems thinking and business transformation world holding a position at the Wharton School of the University of Pennsylvania for decades. His body of work is extensive and includes, among many books, papers, and articles, *Re-creating the Corporation*, *Redesigning Society*, and *Idealized Design*.

2   *Project Management Book of Knowledge, 5th Edition*, The Project Management Institute, page 3.

3   Originally cited in a study dated 1976. Re-cited in a GAO report 21 years later making the point that this was not fixed. *Airport Development Needs: Estimating Future Costs*, United States General Accounting Office (GAO), GAO/RCED-97-99, April 7, 1997.

4   Merrow, Edward W. *Understanding the Outcomes of Megaprojects: A Quantitative Analysis of Very Large Civilian Projects*. RAND Corporation, Santa Monica, California, 1988.

5   *Setting New Standards*, UK government procurement document. Cm 2840 – 1995, 1995.

6   *World Bank. World Bank: US Interests Supported but Oversight Needed to Help Ensure Improved Performance,* US GAO, GAO/NSIAD-96-212, September 1996.

7   "The Business Stake in Effective Project Systems", The Business Roundtable, Washington, DC September 1997, pg. 4.

8   *Dams and Development: A New Framework for Decision-making,* The World Commission on Dams, November 16, 2000: http://www.damsreport.org.

9   PWC quoted in article below (note 10)

10   HBR study quoted by: Hardy-Valle, Benoit, "The Cost of Bad Project Management", *Gallup Business Journal*, February 7, 2012: http://www.gallup.com/businessjournal/152429/cost-bad-project-management.aspx

11   *Spotlight on Oil & Gas Megaprojects*, Ernst & Young, 2014

12   The Project Management Institute, www.pmi.org

13   Barabba, Vincent, Pourdehnad, John, and Russell L. Ackoff, "On misdirecting management", *Strategy & Leadership*, Vol. 30 Issue: 5, pp.5-9, 2002

[14] Based upon the Complex Systems Model of an Organization by Cleland, David I. and King, William R. *Systems Analysis and Project Management, 3rd Edition.* McGraw-Hill, NY, 1983, pg. 23.

[15] Bommer, Michael, DeLaPorte, Renee, and Higgins, James. "Skunkworks Approach to Project Management". *Journal of Management in Engineering.* January, 2002. pps. 21-28.

[16] *Integrated Project Delivery: A Guide,* The American Institute of Architects (AIA), 2007.

[17] Griffith, A.F. and Gibson, G.E., "Alignment During Pre-project Planning", *Journal of Engineering in Management,* April 2001. pps. 69-76.

[19] Jackson, Michael, *Systems Approaches to Management,* 2007, page 239

[20] Ackoff, Russell L., "A Brief Guide to Interactive Planning and Idealized Design", white paper, May 31, 2001.

OTHER WORKS CONSULTED

Works by Russel L. Ackoff:

Re-creating the Corporation, Oxford University Press, 1999.

Idealized Design (with Jason Magidson and Herbert J. Addison), Wharton School Publishing, 2006.

Key Articles:

Magidson, Jason, "Shifting Your Customers into 'Wish Mode': Tools for Generating New Product Ideas and Breakthroughs", Chapter 9 (pps. 235-268) of *The PDMA Toolbook 2 for New Product Development*, John Wiley & Sons, 2004.

Pourdehnad, John and Steele, Mark D., "Re-creating the Capital Project: A Social Systemic Approach", 2nd International Conference on Systems Thinking in Management, University of Salford, UK, 2002.

Steele, Mark D., "Transforming project Organizations Through Systems Thinking", 3rd International Conference on Systems Thinking in Management, University of Pennsylvania, 2004.

ABOUT THE AUTHOR

Mr. Steele is an experienced engineer and consultant based out of the Philadelphia area with over twenty-nine years of experience in engineering, construction, and management across a range of industries including power and utilities, public sector, infrastructure, life sciences, commercial, healthcare, and manufacturing. He has worked closely with senior executives to evaluate project status and risk, assess contract and process compliance, develop recovery plans, negotiate contracts, and create effective project management processes and organizations. Mr. Steele also has extensive litigation experience related to the analysis and preparation of or defense against construction claims related to schedule delays, cost overruns, productivity losses, and design errors and omissions for both public and private sector projects. Mr. Steele is a graduate of West Point and a combat veteran of the US Army. In addition, he is a licensed Professional Engineer, a Certified Cost Professional, and holds a Masters from Villanova University.

He is the principal and founder of Quintain Project Solutions LLC and he can be reached at: msteele@quintainprojectsolutions.com